THE FORGOTTEN

ALSO BY BEN BRADLEE JR.

The Ambush Murders: The True Account of the Killing of Two California Policemen

Prophet of Blood: The Untold Story of Ervil Lebaron and the Lambs of God (with Dale Van Atta)

Guts and Glory: The Rise and Fall of Oliver North

The Kid: The Immortal Life of Ted Williams

THE FORGOTTEN

How the People of
One Pennsylvania County
Elected Donald Trump and
Changed America

BEN BRADLEE JR.

Little, Brown and Company

New York Boston London

Little, Brown and Company
Hachette Book Group
1290 Avenue of the Americas, New York, NY 10104
littlebrown.com

First Edition: October 2018

Little, Brown and Company is a division of Hachette Book Group, Inc. The Little, Brown name and logo are trademarks of Hachette Book Group, Inc.

The publisher is not responsible for websites (or their content) that are not owned by the publisher.

The Hachette Speakers Bureau provides a wide range of authors for speaking events. To find out more, go to hachettespeakersbureau.com or call (866) 376-6591.

All photographs were provided by the people depicted in each image, except for the photographs of Donna Kowalczyk and Ed Harry, which were taken by the author.

ISBN 978-0-316-51573-3
LCCN 2018947607

10 9 8 7 6 5 4 3 2 1

LSC-H

Printed in the United States of America

For Cynthia

CONTENTS

Pennsylvania

LUZERNE COUNTY

PITTSBURGH

PHILADELPHIA

THE FORGOTTEN

AUTHOR'S NOTE

LIKE MANY OTHERS, I was captivated by the improbable political rise of Donald J. Trump and then, even more improbably, by his election as president of the United States.

Here was the best political story in generations: a crude, louche real estate magnate and reality TV star burst on the political scene and dared to say outrageous things that would have meant the end for any other candidate. But Trump, incredibly, seemed to gain strength with each scandalous affront: during his 2015 announcement speech, he accused Mexico of sending "rapists" to America; he shamelessly led the charge in questioning President Barack Obama's U.S. citizenship; just weeks before the election, he weathered the release of the *Access Hollywood* tape in which he boasted in a 2005 secret recording of using his celebrity as license to randomly kiss and grope women; and during the campaign, he fended off charges from eighteen named women that he sexually assaulted or harassed them over the years.

There were other *scandales,* but none of them seemed to

hurt him or matter much. As Trump himself famously said during the campaign, "I could stand in the middle of Fifth Avenue and shoot somebody, and I wouldn't lose any voters, okay? It's, like, incredible!"

Trump steamrolled over his sixteen Republican primary opponents, assigning many of them cruel and demeaning nicknames as he warmed up to face "Crooked Hillary" Clinton in the general election. He was not afraid to touch, even linger on, political third rails like misogyny, xenophobia, anti-Semitism, and race—or to press his signature issue linked to race: rolling back illegal immigration. His shrewd slogan, "Make America Great Again," was a nostalgic paean to a simpler, whiter time in America, when the pace of social change produced little angst. It was a time when what can be seen today as tribalism based on politically incorrect notions of who is and is not an American could thrive unabated.

The Trump story was so rich on so many levels that for a writer, the main problem was where to begin a book—what approach to take.

The overriding questions seemed to be who, exactly, voted for Trump, and why? I began to look more closely at the three Rust Belt swing states where the election had been decided: Pennsylvania, Michigan, and Wisconsin. Surprisingly, Trump won those three states by a total of 77,689 votes out of the more than thirteen million cast. If Hillary Clinton had won them, *she* would have become president.

The three states are overwhelmingly white and had been historically Democratic. Neither Pennsylvania nor Michigan had voted for a Republican for president since 1988—and Wisconsin not since 1984.

But it was Pennsylvania that was the most important of the three because it had the most electoral votes—twenty—and because Clinton, who had family ties to the state, had put it firmly in her column and considered it perhaps her most critical fire wall.

A closer examination of the Pennsylvania vote revealed that Trump won largely on the strength of his showing in the northeast part of the state, and it was one county—Luzerne—that led the way. Trump routed Clinton there by 26,237 votes—a margin of nearly twenty points. His victory represented an abrupt shift in political sentiment, given that President Obama won the traditionally Democratic county by eight percentage points in 2008 and by five points in 2012.

Since Luzerne—home to economically depressed Wilkes-Barre, near Scranton—provided Trump with nearly 60 percent of his winning margin in the state, it is not a stretch to say that this single county won Trump Pennsylvania—and perhaps the presidency, to the extent that the state's demographics and voting patterns were similar to Michigan's and Wisconsin's.

My curiosity piqued, I decided to visit Luzerne and talk to a range of Trump voters about the choices they made. I wanted to see if the county might be a prism through which to explore the underlying reasons for one of the most shocking election results in political history.

I made my first visit on December 6, 2016, less than a month after the election, and over the next fourteen months I would make four more trips lasting up to a week at a time. Initially, I did what reporters do: read as much as I could about the place to absorb its historical background, learned who the leading public officials and community leaders were so I could use them as guideposts, and then plunged in.

During that first visit, people were friendly and welcoming—willing to talk to an outsider, to offer insights about Luzerne County, and to provide the names of Trump voters that I should talk to. I talked to the editor of the *Times Leader,* one of Wilkes-Barre's two daily newspapers, and to his lead political reporter; four of Luzerne's representatives in the state legislature; a Wilkes-Barre city councilman and local historian; and a leading radio talk show host known for having her finger on the county's political pulse.

These people and others helped lead me to a range of Trump voters across Luzerne who seemed to represent a solid cross section of the president's constituency. After interviewing nearly a hundred people over the time that I was in the county, I decided to tell the stories of a dozen in depth—people who I thought collectively revealed much about Trump's appeal, or who represented key portions of his following. To be sure, there was no scientific basis for choosing those I decided to feature. Mostly it was my subjective judgment about the degree to which they served as Trump voter exemplars, as well as the strength of their stories and how they told them.

Each one of these people is different, but their lives share common themes. They have a contempt for Washington and the powers that be, who they feel have mostly abandoned them and left them marginalized by flat or falling wages, rapid demographic change, and a dominant liberal culture that mocks their faith and patriotism. They feel like everyone's punching bag, and that their way of life is dying. They sense a loss of dignity and stature. They feel as though others are cutting in line, and that government is taking too much money from the employed and giving it to the able-bodied idle. They feel that government regulations have become strangling to small and large businesses, and that the country is in danger of being inundated by immigrants—legal and illegal.

A recent surge in the Hispanic population of Luzerne County made Trump's raw immigration pitch relevant and attractive to many voters. For them, the new arrivals sparked not just a yearning for a whiter yesteryear, but an inclination—implicitly encouraged by Trump—to make clear that they preferred to be among their own race and social group. They felt that the place they had lived their whole lives was changing in ways they didn't like or fully understand.

These fears had long been harbored yet usually went unmentioned. But Trump connected strongly to his aggrieved constituency, especially when he called them "the forgotten people." That struck a chord, and then the floodgates seemed to open to him. Trump was able to activate, own, and even weaponize the resentments that Luzerne residents had over issues that were long-standing and hard to solve, if not intractable.

The phrase "the forgotten" implied that there were winners and losers. While other parts of the country have thrived in recent years under globalization and the dizzying pace of technological change, Trump voters in Luzerne and many similar places throughout the land felt dealt out of the prosperity pie, left behind, and generally unacknowledged and unappreciated. They felt relegated to the sidelines, as if their stories didn't matter.

And by whom did they feel forgotten? By the government and the two major political parties. Less discussed was the extent to which those three institutions might have been relatively easy scapegoats, and how much the forgotten's own personal decisions may have contributed to their frustrations in life.

So who, actually, are the people of Luzerne County who played such a pivotal role in Trump's winning Pennsylvania and thus the presidency? There is value in listening to their stories, in considering the ground truths of their daily lives, in understanding what drives them and why they voted the way they did.

They are *The Congressman*. In 2006, Lou Barletta, as the mayor of Hazleton, Luzerne County's second largest city, started a fierce debate about illegal immigration that played itself out nationally and served as a precursor to Trump's candidacy based on the same issue ten years later. Now a congressman representing Luzerne who this year is running for the U.S. Senate against Democratic incumbent Bob Casey, Barletta was cochair of Trump's Pennsylvania campaign and played a key role in Trump's winning the state.

They are *Trump Men* like Vito DeLuca, a self-described Reagan Democrat and lawyer in Luzerne County; Marty Beccone, a registered Independent who owns a bar and restaurant in Hazleton; Ed Harry, a former labor organizer and lifelong Democrat who defied his Clinton-endorsing union leadership when he announced that he was supporting Trump; and Brian Langan, newly retired after working as a detective with the Pennsylvania State Police for more than twenty-five years.

They are *Trump Women* like Lynette Villano, a widow and clerk for a wastewater treatment plant who was enamored with Donald Trump from day one; Donna Kowalczyk, who owns a Wilkes-Barre hair salon and fights to save the street where she lives from further blight and decay; Kim Woodrosky—born into a family of Democrats, her father a teamster and her mother a line worker in a textile mill—who became a successful real estate investor; and Tiffany Cloud, a politically active housewife and former advertising executive who's married to an ex–Army Special Operations officer who did three tours of combat duty.

They are *The Veteran*. Vets like Tiffany's husband, Erik Olson—who did two tours in Iraq and one in Afghanistan—voted for Trump over Clinton by a margin of two to one nationally. Erik never considered Hillary Clinton an option and warmed to Trump gradually. He was turned off by some of his rhetorical excesses but liked his strong leadership and his vision for the country. The gauzy memories evoked by Trump's "Make America Great Again" slogan appealed to Olson too.

They are *The White Nationalist*. Steve Smith, a strapping truck driver from Pittston, heads the Wilkes-Barre/Scranton chapter of Keystone United, a Pennsylvania "white rights" group. An avowed white supremacist, Smith received national attention in 2012 when he was elected as a write-in to the Luzerne County Republican Committee, and then got re-elected by sixty-nine votes in 2016, thereby vaulting from the white extremist underground into the local political mainstream. In an era of identity politics, the phrase "white identity" has become more acceptable during the presidency of Donald Trump. Smith finds Pennsylvania—which now has the fifth highest number of hate groups in the country, along with a KKK presence in Wilkes-Barre—hospitable to his goal of getting whites to assert themselves more aggressively as America's minority population increases. And he is thrilled by the election of Trump, who he says has been a godsend for the white nationalist message.

They are *The Christian*. Though Luzerne is predominantly Catholic, there is a significant and growing evangelical community. Nationwide, evangelicals went 80 percent for Trump in the election and made up nearly half of his total vote. One of Trump's most ardent Christian followers is Jessica Harker, a registered nurse who works for the U.S. Department of Veterans Affairs in Wilkes-Barre. She calls herself "on fire" for the Lord, and freely mixes in scripture as she speaks while not shying away from saltier, earthly language. She believes that God chose Trump to be president.

All these people are white, as Trump's voters overwhelmingly were. And they are older than forty-five—again, as were most of Trump's voters.

And finally, there are *The Democrats*—minorities and white liberals left behind to navigate an uneasy coexistence with still-euphoric Trump supporters, who well recognize the key role they played in delivering Pennsylvania to the president, and who sometimes still can't resist spiking the football about it.

With much of the country still stunned that a candidate as unusual as Trump got elected president, *The Forgotten* uses Luzerne County as a way to more closely examine the white working and middle class that served as the backbone of Trump's support throughout the United States. These detailed portraits of a group of disillusioned voters, writ large, tell much of the story of the 2016 election, and offer important lessons—both for the upcoming midterm elections, which will largely be a referendum on the Trump presidency to date, and for the future of the country.

Ben Bradlee Jr., July 2, 2018

INTRODUCTION

SINCE MIDSUMMER OF 2016, it looked as though Pennsylvania might be the tipping point in the presidential election, because it personified the economic pain changing the politics of the older industrial states.

Trump's unconventional candidacy was premised in large part on his ability to persuade blue-collar and white working-class Democrats to cross over to the Republican Party. He made opposition to immigration, globalization, and what he believed were poorly negotiated trade deals a central argument in his campaign. People concerned about the economic deterioration of Pennsylvania, and particularly places like Luzerne County, were ripe for Trump. A swing, bellwether county, Luzerne has almost perfectly matched the rest of Pennsylvania's vote in every presidential election since 2000.

Luzerne seemed especially open to Trump's nationalist, economic message: he had won a whopping 77 percent of the county's vote (and 57 percent statewide) in Pennsylvania's

April Republican primary, swamping his remaining opponents, Texas senator Ted Cruz and Ohio governor John Kasich.

The day before the primary, Trump attracted an overflow crowd of some twelve thousand people to Mohegan Sun Arena, outside Wilkes-Barre. The rally was a revelation of sorts for many local residents—some of whom had been embarrassed to express their public support for the turbulent and contentious candidate. Now folks attending the rally could see Trump's hidden vote start to come out of the closet, and they could witness firsthand how many of their friends and neighbors really felt about him: they seemed smitten.

On October 10, one month before the election, Trump returned to the same arena for another jam-packed rally, this one even more raucous and filled with energy. The crowd was more economically diverse than the one in April: it was still primarily blue-collar, but with plenty of middle-class and some upper-middle-class residents represented as well. One VIP took note: Vice President Joe Biden, who had been raised twenty miles north, in Scranton, had drawn a fraction of Trump's crowds while campaigning in the area for Clinton. When Biden saw video clips of the Wilkes-Barre rally showing how the crowd was responding to Trump, he later told the *Los Angeles Times* that he said to himself, "Son of a gun. We may lose this election."

And they did.

Luzerne County has about 320,000 people and spans 907 square miles—big enough to squeeze in the entire state of

Rhode Island. Interstates 80 and 81 intersect in the county, and Philadelphia and New York City are each about a two-hour drive away. Though a mix of urban and rural, Luzerne is covered by parts of the Appalachian mountain range and is on the whole more rural in character. While there are pockets of well-heeled suburbia, Luzerne is less Northeast Corridor than Appalachia.

Like many other counties in the industrial North and Midwest, Luzerne has been in economic distress for decades due to the demise of the coal industry that was once its anchor, and also due to the loss of thousands of manufacturing jobs that replaced coal. As a result, the social fabric has been frayed by a high unemployment rate and low-wage jobs, crime, and a surging opioid epidemic. In addition, new and added tensions have been created by a spike in immigration, mostly by Hispanics. Eighty-three percent of the population remains white, 11 percent is Hispanic, and 5 percent is black.

The county has been a Democratic stronghold since the 1960s, with its working-class, union-affiliated population. It hadn't voted for a Republican president since 1988, but there had been signs that the days of Democratic domination were coming to an end. Luzerne now lines up more closely with the demographic profile of Western Pennsylvania: older, whiter voters who have seen good-paying jobs disappear and not return.

Trump's winning majority in Luzerne exceeded President Obama's thirty-thousand-vote swing from 2012, when he won the county by five thousand votes. Obama also won Luzerne in 2008. But many Democrats who supported

Obama twice decided to make the leap to a much different kind of candidate in Trump.

"Obama had hope and change, Trump had knock-down-the-door and change," says John Yudichak, a Democrat who represents Luzerne County in the Pennsylvania state senate. Yudichak says he went to Trump's April rally in Wilkes-Barre and asked a union prison guard why he was with Trump.

"The man replied, 'Donald Trump makes me feel good about myself and who I am. Hillary makes me apologize if I want to hunt and don't have a college education.'" Yudichak adds that 85 percent of his district consists of "uneducated white voters," meaning those who have not gone to college. "I would hear TV pundits use that phrase all the time. That was attacking the dignity of people that go to work every day," Yudichak says. "People felt left behind and felt the deck was stacked against them. When Trump used the word 'rigged,' that resonated."

The campaign of Donald Trump exposed a gulf of culture and class that fell largely on rural-versus-urban fault lines. The election results can mostly be seen as the revenge of the rural voter. The rural poor, the working class, and the middle class felt largely ignored and condescended to by the Democratic Party, and Trump galvanized those voters' long-simmering frustrations. Electing Trump was a rebuke of globalization and the unseen ruling classes and elites who had changed his voters' lives without their consent.

The final 2016 presidential election results, county by county, look like a landslide for Trump.

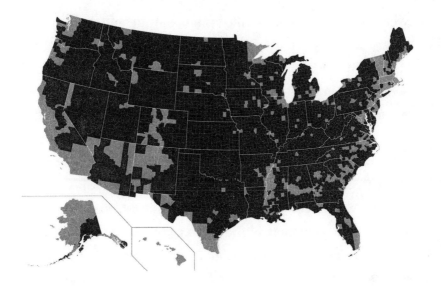

The people who live in the vast middle of the United States have felt largely neglected. The election was less about the cities than it was about the individual counties across the nation: self-governing units with their own police, firemen, school systems, and municipal services. Many counties have urban centers, but most, like Luzerne, are rural in character, and some can serve as a microcosm of America.

While much of the red-blue divide can be linked to festering cultural differences and antagonisms, there was an economic split as well. A postelection Brookings Institution analysis found that the 493 counties that Hillary Clinton won were in heavily metropolitan areas that generate 64 percent of America's economic activity, as measured by total output in 2015. By contrast, the 2,584 counties that Trump won, in rural and exurban parts of the country, produce just 36 percent of the country's output. So another way to look at the election is as a reflection of the chasm that exists between what Brookings called high-output and low-output America.

After the election, much the same way that Jane Goodall studies chimpanzees in the wild, social scientists and out-of-touch Democrats launched anthropologic-like surveys on the white working class. Clinton had largely ignored this key group during the campaign, instead trying to replicate the Obama coalition of minorities, millennials, suburban women, and the white, college-educated professional class. Some of the motivating factors behind Trump's appeal could be found in an anonymous, postelection email circulating among his voters in Luzerne County and elsewhere; its candid sentiments amounted to a Trump voters' creed.

I haven't said too much about this election since the start . . . but this is how I feel . . . I'm noticing that a lot of you aren't graciously accepting the fact that your candidate lost. In fact, you seem to be posting even more hateful things about those of us who voted for Trump. Some of you are apparently "triggered" because you are posting how "sick" you feel about the results. How did this happen, you ask?

You created "us" when you attacked our freedom of speech. You created "us" when you attacked our right to bear arms. You created "us" when you attacked our Christian beliefs. You created "us" when you constantly referred to us as racists. You created "us" when you constantly called us xenophobic. You created "us" when you told us to get on board or get out of the way. You created "us" when you attacked our flag. You created "us" when you took God out of our schools. You created "us" when you confused women's rights with feminism. You created "us" when you began to emasculate men. You created "us" when you decided to make our children soft. You created "us" when you decided to vote for progressive ideals. You created "us" when you attacked our way of life. You created "us" when you decided to let our government get out of control. You created "us," the silent majority. You created "us" when you began murdering innocent law enforcement officers. You created "us" when you lied and said we could keep our insurance plans and our doctors. You created "us" when you allowed our jobs to continue to leave our country. You created "us" when you took a knee, or stayed seated or didn't remove your hat during our national anthem. You created "us" when you forced us to buy health care and then financially penalized us for not participating.

And we became fed up and we pushed back and spoke up. And we did it with ballots, not bullets. With ballots, not riots. With ballots, not looting.

With ballots, not blocking traffic. With ballots, not fires, except the one you started inside of "us."

YOU created "US." It really is just that simple.

Perhaps the most telling revelations to emerge from exit poll interviews of people who cast ballots in the 2016 election were the defection of millions of white working-class voters—almost one in four—who had voted for Obama in 2012 but jumped to Trump in 2016, and Trump's dominance of the white vote generally, especially among whites who did not go to college. Trump won white voters, who made up 69 percent of the electorate, by twenty-one points, fifty-eight to thirty-seven, one point higher than Mitt Romney's fifty-nine to thirty-nine margin in 2012. White men voted 63 percent for

Trump and 31 percent for Clinton, while Trump also carried white women, fifty-three to forty-three. Among white women without college degrees, Trump beat Clinton by twenty-eight points. In total, women supported Clinton over Trump fifty-four to forty-two, the same twelve-point margin by which Trump defeated Clinton among men. Given the disparaging comments Trump had made about women, as well as the sexual assault or harassment allegations made against him by eighteen women during the campaign,[1] many had predicted there would be a surge of new women voters going to the polls to vote against him. But nothing of the sort materialized: women made up 52 percent of the overall vote in 2016, down a point from 53 percent in 2012.

There was a wide gap in presidential preferences between those with a college degree and those without. College grads backed Clinton, fifty-two to forty-three, while non-college-educated voters supported Trump, fifty-two to forty-four. But among whites without a college degree, Trump's margin was the largest recorded in exit polls since 1980. Trump overwhelmed Clinton among voters in this category by thirty-nine points, sixty-seven to twenty-eight. Trump also won whites with a college degree, but by only four points, forty-nine to forty-five.

It was a change election. Among the 39 percent of voters who said that supporting a candidate who could "bring needed change" was their top priority, 83 percent chose Trump and 14 percent opted for Clinton. The change impulse was so compelling it apparently overrode concerns about Trump personally. Only 38 percent of voters had a favorable view of him, 35 percent said he had the temperament to serve effectively as president, 38 percent said he was qualified, while just a third called him "honest and trustworthy."[2]

Digging deeper into the Trump vote, the Democracy Fund, a bipartisan foundation established by eBay founder Pierre Omidyar, conducted a postelection survey of eight thousand voters in partnership with the market research firm YouGov. The results suggested that there were five types of Trump voters. The two most statistically significant constituencies were what the study called American Preservationists, representing 20 percent of the total, and Anti-Elites, at 19 percent.

American Preservationists were "the core Trump constituency that propelled him to victory in the early Republican primaries... [and which] believe the economic and political systems are rigged, have nativist immigration views, and a nativist and ethnocultural conception of American identity"—in other words, a white conception of American citizenship. The Preservationists have a strong sense of their racial and Christian identity, oppose not just illegal but also legal immigration, and vehemently supported Trump's plan for a temporary Muslim travel ban. They are angry about race relations and believe there is as much discrimination against whites as against minorities, and they believe that "real Americans need to have been born in America or have lived here most of their lives and be Christian."

The Anti-Elites, for their part, believe "that moneyed and political elites take advantage of the system against ordinary people" and support raising taxes on the rich. They too believe that the system is rigged, but they take more moderate positions on race, immigration, and American identity than the Preservationists do, and they are more willing to compromise.

The three other types of Trump voters were two traditional Republican groups, labeled Staunch Conservatives (31 percent) and Free Marketeers (25 percent), and a final group merely called the Disengaged. The Staunch Conservatives are steadfast fiscal conservatives who "embrace moral traditionalism." They are the most loyal Republican voters, and the most likely to own guns and be NRA members. The Free Marketeers are described as being "free traders with moderate to liberal positions on immigration and race," and their vote was primarily motivated by being against Clinton rather than for Trump. Finally, the Disengaged are defined as not knowing much about politics and feeling detached from institutions.[3]

Luzerne County had been drifting from its Democratic union roots for years, and found itself open to Trump's America First agenda, his call for a stronger border with Mexico, and his tough pro-gun and anti-abortion positions.

In 2016, 5,643 Luzerne Democrats switched to the Republican Party so they could vote in the GOP primary—the vast majority of them for Trump. This party shift was the largest in either direction by any Pennsylvania county other than Philadelphia and Allegheny. Trump tailored his simple, populist message to the region's working-class voters, who felt left out and overlooked—"the forgotten people," as Trump called them.

When Barack Obama was campaigning for president during the recession of 2008, he made what was thought at the time to have been an impolitic remark about people living in the T section of Pennsylvania, the more conservative area between Pittsburgh and Philadelphia that the political consultant James Carville once famously likened to Alabama.

In April 2008, then-senator Obama—speaking to a wealthy crowd at a San Francisco fund-raiser two weeks before the Pennsylvania primary, in which he was in a close race with Hillary Clinton—said the following: "You go into some of these small towns in Pennsylvania and, like a lot of small towns in the Midwest, the jobs have been gone now for twenty-five years and nothing's replaced them. And they fell through the Clinton administration, and the Bush administration, and each successive administration has said that somehow these communities are going to regenerate, and they have not. So it's not surprising then that they get bitter, and they cling to guns or religion or antipathy toward people who aren't like them, or anti-immigrant sentiment, or anti-trade sentiment as a way to explain their frustrations."

Clinton jumped on the remark and called Obama an "elitist." The fuss may have helped her in the short term since she won the Pennsylvania primary, but she went on to lose the Democratic nomination to the young senator from Illinois.

Yet in hindsight, it's apparent that what Obama said was essentially true, and seven years later, as president, he circled back to the remarks in the context of Trump's appeal to the white working class in places like Luzerne County. In a December 2015 interview with National Public Radio, Obama reaffirmed his 2008 comments, citing "demographic change with all the economic stresses that people have been going through because of the financial crisis, because of technology, because of globalization, the fact that wages and incomes have been flatlining for some time, and that particularly blue-collar men have had a lot of trouble in this new economy. You combine those things, and it means that there is going to be potential anger, frustration, fear. Some of it justified, but just misdirected. I think somebody like Mr. Trump is taking advantage of that. That's what he's exploiting during the course of his campaign."

Another way of thinking about Trump voters was to say that they were, in the words of the *Wall Street Journal*'s Peggy Noonan, "the unprotected."

"There are the protected and the unprotected," she wrote in a 2016 column, eight months before the election. "The protected make public policy. The unprotected live in it. The unprotected are starting to push back, powerfully. The protected are the accomplished, the secure, the successful—those who have power or access to it. They are protected from much of the roughness of the world. More to the point, they are protected *from the world they have created* . . . The unprotected came to think they owed the establishment—another word for the protected—nothing, no particular loyalty, no old allegiance. Mr. Trump came from that."[4]

Tony Brooks, the lone Republican on the Wilkes-Barre city council and a Luzerne County historian, thinks another way to look at the 2016 campaign is as a struggle between "the givers and the takers."

"And the givers are fed up with the takers," Brooks says. "Every single block in Wilkes-Barre will have a row of houses that are immaculate—generally retired, white working class, and union. Cut grass and a tomato garden in the back. But sadly, within the last twenty years, we've seen a lot of what I call economic refugees from New York and New Jersey who have moved in under Section 8 housing. So, one house sits pristine and immaculate next to another on Section 8. The people in the nice house feel like their investment is going down the tubes. And they connected this feeling to Donald Trump. They'll say, 'I'm not a racist: it's because he's a bad neighbor, with trash on his front porch.' This is happening in other Rust Belt cities across America. People were frustrated by so many takers in their neighborhood. And not giving back. Living on the dole. They saw themselves as giving, paying their taxes while their neighbors were not. And they attached that to the entitlement mind-set of the Democratic Party."

There were earlier cultural and political touchstones that paved the way for Trump.

One was Morton Downey Jr.'s television talk show of the late eighties, which served as a petri dish for the tumultuous Trump rallies that sustained his campaign, and from which he has continued to draw oxygen as president.

"Downey, who died in 2001, presided over the original Trump rally," wrote Charles McElwee, a Luzerne County historian, in a 2017 article for the *American Conservative* that examined the links between Downey and Trump. "His show launched during the final stretch of Reagan's presidency, a period of cataclysmic change in the media realm that was only realized in hindsight...Downey's show developed a loyal cult following. His confrontational persona, distinguished by an intolerance for excessive political correctness, especially resonated with a large segment of the increasingly postindustrial mid-Atlantic...

"They cultivated a base of aggrieved Republicans and Democrats who once cheered at Downey's crude insults and now laugh at Trump's stinging tweets...The modern working-class Americans who appreciate Downey or Trump fail to click with either political party. They're just navigating the frantic pace of a global economy that often appears to present little hope for their future. In 1987, their outlet for populist release was Downey's show. Now it's Trump's presidency."[5]

A political forerunner of Trump was Pat Buchanan, the archconservative former adviser to Presidents Nixon, Ford, and Reagan who became a TV commentator and syndicated columnist, and unsuccessfully sought the Republican presidential nominations in 1992 and 1996 while running as a populist.

It was Buchanan who warned some twenty-five years before Trump that the United States was losing its global stature; who questioned how much the United States should pay for the defense of its allies; who promoted an America First agenda, excoriated both the Republican and Democratic parties for leaving working-class Americans behind, and railed against the effects of globalization and multiculturalism. Buchanan also drew on the racial resentments and anti-elitist scorn of George Wallace, as did Trump, who first made himself politically prominent and viable for the Republican nomination by fanning nativist flames over the issue of Obama's birth certificate: Could Obama prove he had really been born in Hawaii, or was even an American?

The loss of some five million manufacturing jobs since 2000, coupled with stagnant incomes, caused a bubbling anger that—along with the rise of talk radio and cable networks and the powerful emergence of social media—turned Trump's campaign into Buchanan's on steroids.[6]

Trump's "Make America Great Again" campaign slogan was a skillful and evocative use of nostalgia that invited his base to conjure up a placid and white *Ozzie and Harriet*–like vista of American life in the 1950s, before the immigrant hordes arrived. Trump co-opted the slogan from Ronald Reagan, who first used "*Let's* make America great again" in his 1980 campaign, when the country's economy was lagging. Bill Clinton also used the line in his 1992 campaign, though in speeches, not as a slogan.

As for Trump's phrase "the forgotten people"—the people he said he was fighting for—it echoed Franklin Roosevelt's 1932 speech about "the forgotten man at the bottom of the economic pyramid" and also contained a dash of Huey Long from the same era.

LUZERNE

Forty years I worked with pick and drill,
Down in the mines against my will,
The Coal King's slave, but now it's passed
Thanks be to God, I am free at last.

Inscription on the grave of Condy Breslin at St. Gabriel's
Cemetery in Hazleton, Pennsylvania

CONDY BRESLIN WAS part of a wave of immigrants who fled Donegal, Ireland, and the Irish famine in the nineteenth century for Hazleton, which then sat on the world's richest vein of anthracite coal. Breslin spent years mining the coal, and after inhaling too much of its toxic dust, he died of asthma in 1880.

Following the coal discovery, Hazleton and other parts of Luzerne exploded in growth, and waves of immigrants from Ireland, Italy, Germany, and Eastern Europe flocked to northeast Pennsylvania and the New World to share in whatever crumbs of lucre the coal barons deigned to share with them, which wasn't much.

The immigrants settled in so-called patch towns owned by the coal companies and toiled away in virtual servitude, working long hours in the mines and living in shanties from which they could be evicted at any time. Rents for the shacks were deducted from their wages, along with food and any mining supplies they bought at inflated prices in company stores. Each patch town usually had a saloon and a Protestant church, thanks to the influence of the Welsh, who had been the first of the European immigrants to arrive in the Wyoming Valley, which surrounds Wilkes-Barre. By the turn of the twentieth century, however, Roman Catholics had established a clear plurality in the county.

To help satisfy an increasing demand for coal, the mining companies began to use child labor, or "breaker boys," who were usually sons of the immigrants. Working conditions in the mines were frightful, and there were frequent deaths. When a miner died, the companies would wrap up his body in a sack and unceremoniously drop it off at his home for his family to deal with.

In the late 1860s, the Workingmen's Benevolent Association established the first union of anthracite coal miners. In addition, groups of Irish immigrants sympathetic to the plight of their countrymen working in deplorable conditions in the Pennsylvania mines offered physical and moral support to their brethren. They supported miners who wanted to keep working rather than enlist in the Civil War (coal barons saw conscription as a way to break up the agitators) and assisted in combatting discrimination against the Irish and against Catholics. Some of the Irish immigrants were either sympathetic to, or members of, the Molly Maguires, a secret society that instigated agrarian violence against landowners in rural Ireland, and they launched attacks against mine bosses, including beatings and murders.

The Coal and Iron Police—a private security force that Pennsylvania's general assembly had authorized the mining companies to create—worked to counter the union organizing activity. Separately, the coal operators hired detectives from the Pinkerton Agency to fight fire with fire against the Irish security forces and some transplanted Molly Maguires who established a beachhead in Pennsylvania. The Catholic Church, meanwhile, struck an alliance with the coal companies by threatening to excommunicate the Mollys, thereby weakening the group further. Finally, twenty Mollys were convicted of murder and various other crimes, and then executed by hanging between 1877 and 1879. Ten of the men were hung on one day, June 21, 1877, "Black Thursday," in neighboring Schuylkill and Carbon counties, an event that remains etched deeply in Pennsylvania folklore.[1]

As miners began to grow more restless at their dire circumstances, they initiated labor disputes that often resulted in further violence. In 1897, striking miners marching outside Hazleton while unarmed were massacred by a Luzerne County sheriff's posse. Nineteen men were killed and thirty-two others wounded—a shocking event that helped pave the way for unionizing efforts led by the United Mine Workers. Subsequent strikes in 1900 and 1902 yielded significant wage increases and improved working conditions for the miners.

In the coal industry's heyday, from 1875 to 1955, Wilkes-Barre—Luzerne's county seat, straddling the redoubtable Susquehanna River—was known as Pennsylvania's third city, often mediating disputes between its much larger neighbors to the east and west, Philadelphia and Pittsburgh. Wilkes-Barre dominated the rural, northern, and central parts of the state between the two big cities on either side.

"We used to be the Saudi Arabia of coal," says the Wilkes-Barre historian Tony Brooks. At its peak in 1930, Wilkes-Barre had a population of eighty-nine thousand. It's less than half that now.

The power of coal began to wane with competition from oil and gas, but in 1959, the Knox mine disaster in Pittston virtually ended coal in Luzerne County. Twelve miners were drowned when water from the Susquehanna burst into the many interconnected mine galleries in the Wyoming Valley.

Coal miners did not want their kids to be miners, and by and large they weren't. Many went to college and moved away. This trend started after World War I and escalated after World War II, resulting in a significant youth brain drain, which continues to this day. "So, politics for the last fifty years has been about fighting over what's left," says Brooks.

Though parents naturally want the best for their children, when the younger generation does move away in search of better opportunity, there can be a lingering sense of resentment on the part of friends and family left behind in Luzerne. "It's a sense of, 'Who does he think he is?'" says Charles

McElwee, the county historian, who is an economic development specialist for the nonprofit Community Area New Development Organization in Hazleton.

Welsh Republicans dominated local politics from the Civil War to 1960, as Wilkes-Barre and Scranton were the leading destinations for Welsh immigration. The coal barons built stately mansions along the Susquehanna, as well as magnificent public buildings like the Luzerne County Courthouse.

Though Democrats held power statewide and in Luzerne County during the FDR years, Republicans regained sway with the outbreak of World War II, and by 1946, they had a registration advantage over Democrats by some eighty-three thousand voters.[2]

But that changed in 1960, with the election of John F. Kennedy as president. Powered by a huge turnout of ethnic Catholics in Luzerne County, Kennedy defeated Richard Nixon in Pennsylvania by just over a hundred thousand votes. Luzerne was then still the fourth largest county in the state, and though the rural countryside was largely Republican, the cities and patch towns—which held most of the county's population of 346,972—were solidly Democratic.

In a twenty-car motorcade, Kennedy targeted a series of cities and towns in eastern Pennsylvania, from Philadelphia to Scranton. Huge crowds in Allentown and Bethlehem only grew as he headed into the Luzerne County mining country in Hazleton, Nanticoke, Pittston, and Wilkes-Barre. Riding with the flamboyant local congressman Dan Flood in Flood's trademark white Cadillac, Kennedy was mobbed and reportedly shook so many hands that his own hand was bleeding by the end of the day. He drew some thirty-five thousand people late in the afternoon of October 28 in Wilkes-Barre's Public Square, just eleven days before the election.

By the 1970s, following the coal industry's collapse, Luzerne County began a sustained period of population loss. In 1972, Hurricane Agnes caused the Susquehanna to overflow and bury Wilkes-Barre under nine feet of water, dealing the city another economic blow. In the ensuing years, it became largely a city of abandoned buildings and boarded-up storefronts as the remaining residents struggled to find their footing in an economy in which the main employers were now government agencies, local colleges, and hospitals.

"Wilkes-Barre is in the middle of what every Rust Belt town has been going through for the last thirty years: trying to rehabilitate and repurpose itself," says Brooks. "But we're probably a decade behind others of our ilk."

Luzerne had been reliably Democratic in presidential elections for decades, except for a detour to Richard Nixon in 1972, the year he routed George McGovern and carried every state in the country except Massachusetts. The county voted for Jimmy Carter in 1976, but along with the rest of the nation, it tired of him by 1980 and elected Ronald Reagan. Thus began a decade of Republican presidential dominance in the county as thousands of Reagan Democrats crossed over to reelect Reagan in 1984, and to vote for George H. W. Bush in 1988, in hopes that the GOP could reverse the pattern of industrial decline and urban decay that had taken hold in the county.

By 1992, however, Luzerne Democrats decided to come home to a man they hoped would be their new working-class icon: Bill Clinton. Their economic lot had not improved in the Reagan–Bush years, and Clinton's empathetic "I feel your pain" manner seemed like a better bet than four additional years under the aristocratic Bush.

Yet by that time, larger macroeconomic forces were at work that no president—not Clinton nor George W. Bush nor Barack Obama, who each had two terms to work with— could fully control: the emergence of the Internet, along with other exploding advances in technology; the expansion of free trade; the globalization of the economy; and the decline of manufacturing, to name but a few. While all those factors helped lift certain sections of the country, notably the big cities on either coast, they consistently stung Luzerne County, particularly the loss of manufacturing jobs.

Between 1937 and 1962, a thriving garment industry had established itself in Luzerne, with nearly two hundred shirt and dress manufacturers employing ten thousand people— nearly all of them women.[3] The garment factories helped cushion the local economy from the demise of coal. But with the rise of foreign competition, the manufacturing jobs started to disappear as well. Pencil maker Eberhard Faber moved to Mexico in the mid-1980s, and other manufacturing plants closed. Manufacturing has declined by one-third since 2000. At 5.4 percent as of April 2018, the unemployment rate in Luzerne has been higher than the state and national average for years. Many of the jobs remaining are low-paying service jobs in fast-food restaurants and chain stores.

Today more than one in five Luzerne County families with

children live in poverty—five percentage points over the state average, and nine points higher than in 2000. Per capita income hovers under $25,000, about $4,500 less than the state average. Median income has been flat in the county since 2000. The exodus of youth in search of better opportunity elsewhere has left behind an older, more conservative electorate.[4]

Meanwhile, the county's Hispanic population has climbed by a factor of ten since 2000, to thirty-one thousand, adding a layer of strain for the majority whites. The Hispanics are centered in Hazleton, which has a population of about twenty-five thousand and sits on a rolling plateau atop Spring Mountain, nearly two thousand feet above sea level, in the southern part of Luzerne. Hazleton has traditionally felt politically and economically disenfranchised from Wilkes-Barre and the rest of Luzerne. As the county seat, Wilkes-Barre is home to the county courthouse, as well as other county and state offices and nonprofits, so Hazleton feels left out. In the past, it has considered seceding from Luzerne and becoming part of nearby Carbon and Schuylkill counties.

In 2000, Hazleton was still 95 percent white and 5 percent Hispanic, but by 2016, the Hispanic percentage had jumped to 52 and the whites were reduced to 44. Some of the former majority are finding it difficult to adapt, and there is the occasional Confederate flag visible, flying in defiance.[5] Fox News commentator Tucker Carlson took sympathetic note of the white plight in Hazleton recently, telling his viewers, "This is more change than human beings are designed to digest." He asked, "How would you feel if that happened in your neighborhood?"[6]

The new arrivals are primarily second- and third-generation Dominican Americans from New York City, Philadelphia, and northern New Jersey attracted by economic opportunity and a lower cost of living. They tend to keep close ties to their homeland, so candidates seeking national office in the Dominican Republic make campaign stops in Hazleton in an effort to get people to cast absentee ballots for them.

The recession of 2008 only made things in Luzerne worse, and the recovery from that upheaval was spotty at best. There were isolated examples of success, such as attracting warehouse businesses like Amazon, Cargill, and the clothing retailer American Eagle to locate near the intersection of Interstates 80 and 81 in Hazleton, but these companies largely offered minimum wage jobs that didn't support a middle-class life.

By the time of the 2016 presidential campaign, a postindustrial malaise had settled over Luzerne, along with a growing anger and frustration over the tectonic cultural, demographic, and economic shifts that the white working class, at least, seemed ready to assign bipartisan blame to. It was the perfect moment for a nonideological and malleable populist to emerge, a candidate nominally a Republican but who didn't seem wedded to either party: Donald J. Trump.

"In Luzerne, you were dealing with a population that felt politically and economically disenfranchised," says Charles McElwee. "This accumulated over decades. You have continued economic decline. What were once thriving neighborhoods were being overwhelmed by crime, drugs, blight, and people turned to a figure, Trump, who communicated their feelings and frustrations about these trends."

Sue Henry, the leading radio talk show host in the county, on WILK in Wilkes-Barre until she resigned early this year, says that Trump caught on from the start.

"The affinity people here had for Trump was amazing," Henry says. "My listeners said, 'He's our guy.' I said, 'Yes, but he's been married three times.' They didn't care. They never wavered. People were so loyal. They would never give up. It was so amazing to see, here in Wilkes-Barre, a blue-collar Democratic town. It blew my mind that they were going for Trump. They believed they had been left behind—mostly economically."

Larry DeFluri, a retired union steward for the American Federation of State, County, and Municipal Employees, is a hard-core Democrat who cast his first vote outside the party for Trump, and he brought about sixty members of his extended family along with him. "My extended family is very large and when we had a get-together over that summer, everyone was planning to vote for Trump," DeFluri recalls. "All my cousins and their children, their wives. We had about sixty votes right there. Jobs was the driving issue. People here only average about twenty thousand dollars a year. Taxes keep going up. Wages are stagnant."

Joe Dougherty, who manages an automotive paint store in Wilkes-Barre and calls himself a member of the middle class, thinks that "Washington has turned its back on people like me. The Democrats, especially, have been moving away from us. More specifically, eight years of promises under Obama did not get us anywhere. The middle class is shouldering the burden of just about everything. I thought we needed a drastic change. Let's give Trump a chance to shake things up and see what happens."

The Second Amendment was also a key issue for Dougherty, who is fifty-one. "I carry a concealed weapon, so that's very important to me too. I don't want my gun taken from me."

Few do in Luzerne, and the same goes for the rest of Pennsylvania, where guns are sacrosanct, and where schools are canceled on the first day of hunting season so students can take to the woods with their fathers. Older voters especially were convinced that Hillary would have come for their guns had she been elected. That was reason enough for many to vote for Trump.

Aaron Kaufer, a Republican state representative for Luzerne County, thought the election came down to hard pocketbook issues, along with a tinge of resentment against welfare recipients. "It was about saving enough money to buy your own beer," Kaufer says. "People here are sick of having the government buy beer for others."

The part-fact, part-fantasy construct of the welfare queen—first introduced into the American political lexicon by Ronald Reagan in 1976, during his losing Republican primary campaign against Gerald Ford—endures in Luzerne.

"People told me they saw immigrants with welfare cards buying steak and lobster, then getting into their Cadillac Escalades," says Eddie Pashinski, a Democratic state representative for the county. "It may be a myth, but people feel this."

Patrick Umbra, a Wilkes-Barre pro-life activist who regularly prays at abortion clinics and is an active member of the Knights of Columbus, has no patience for those on welfare and blames Democrats for encouraging people to seek out government assistance. "I mean, the jobs around here are pathetic, so if you're working for eight dollars an hour and you have three kids, forget it," Umbra says. "Then you'd rather be on welfare. And that's the situation Obama and the Democrats created: sit around, drink, and have fun. That's not the way to go."

There were plenty of women in Luzerne who voted for Trump, unfazed by his history of denigrating comments about women or by the numerous charges of sexual harassment or assault made against him during the campaign, all of which he denied.

"They kept saying there were no women for Trump, that he embarrassed us and degraded us," says Margaret Phillips, sixty-five, who recently retired as a vice president for a major phone company. "But within Luzerne County, there were plenty of women for Trump. Maybe they were afraid to say so, but they were going to vote for him. Women are a lot smarter than that—at least professionals who feel secure in their life. Hillary and her whole campaign, even the pollsters who had it so wrong—they wanted to create the impression that all women were against Trump."

Phillips mentioned something else that motivated her to vote for Trump: her resentment of elites who she thought were trying to dictate how she and others in the heartland should think. "People were tired of the elites like Obama ridiculing the country and places like Luzerne County."

That is a widespread feeling in Luzerne, where, despite acknowledging many problems in their communities, residents remain proud of where they live.

"I'm proud of this area and I don't like it when metropolitan areas look down on us—whether we voted for Trump or not," says David Pedri, the Luzerne County manager. "I don't like being called a country bumpkin when I'm not."

Pedri, a Democrat, says that he was shocked by the size of Trump's victory margin in the county. Pedri oversees six unions in Luzerne, and when he suggested to one group, the corrections officers, that voting for Trump would be against their economic self-interest, "they said they didn't care. They were all voting for him anyway because it was time to shake things up."

Mark Ricetti, director of operations at the Luzerne County Historical Society, says that Trump pulled people to the polls who hadn't voted in years. "Nixon used to brag that he had the silent majority, and that's what Trump had," says Ricetti, a Libertarian and Wilkes-Barre native whose relatives used to work in the mines. He's a self-described "Wyoming Valley boy" who owns a motor home and drives a race car on weekends. "I know many people who hadn't voted in years and years, because they thought all politicians were the same. But they came out for Trump. They thought that good, bad, or indifferent, it was not going to be business as usual with him. The immigration issue was big. This area has a big distaste for illegal immigration because most of the people in the mines were legal European immigrants."

In fact, Trump's signature issue of illegal immigration effectively merged with his supporters' desire to also curb *legal* immigration, which was changing the complexion of their communities and causing related problems, such as more crime and an unequal burden on property taxes. Trump played on voters' fears and anxieties.

In the 2017 paperback edition of her book *White Trash: The 400-Year Untold History of Class in America,* Nancy Isenberg writes that Trump "tapped into anxieties of all who resented government for handing over the country to supposedly less deserving classes: new immigrants, protesting African Americans, lazy welfare freeloaders, and Obamacare recipients asking for handouts. Angry Trump voters were convinced that these 'takers' were not playing by the rules (i.e., working their way up the ladder) and that government entitlement programs were allowing some to advance past the more deserving (white, native-born) Americans. That is how many came to feel 'disinherited.'"[7]

Trump supporters came to love the candidate's willingness to be proudly defiant of liberal niceties and pieties—to be politically *incorrect.* The term "politically incorrect" has become a tired trope over the years, but there was no doubting its enduring power to attract voters to a man they felt was liberating them to speak their minds, to say publicly what they had long kept bottled up inside for fear of violating social norms, to be a bit *naughty.*

In addition, they identified with Trump's nonpolitical, direct manner of speech.

"Trump's simple, relatable speak, like 'yuge,' 'big league,' or 'bigly,' may have turned off voters in other parts of the country, but it wouldn't surprise me if it helped him connect with this county," says the Trump supporter Tiffany Cloud, who lives near Hazleton. "Many here don't place tremendous value on grammar or eloquence. Plenty who are quite educated use 'youse' as the plural of 'you.' There is great local pride in speaking 'Hazleton speak,' or in the case of Wilkes-Barre, I think it's called '[Wyoming] Valley speak.'"

Luzerne County and northeast Pennsylvania do have a distinctive dialect, jokingly called Heynabonics. The slang word "heyna" is a request for affirmation meaning "Isn't that right?" For instance, "You're going dancing Friday night, heyna?" means "You're going dancing Friday night, right?"[8]

According to a YouTube video on how to speak Heynabonics, the first principle of the dialect is verbal economy, so a question like "Did you eat?" is shortened to simply "J'eat?" Instead of saying the word "several," an instructor in the YouTube sketch advises his class to say "couple two-tree" (not "three"). This usually refers to the number of beers being ordered, the instructor adds. Other examples: The coat is "myan," not "mine." "To" is "ta" and "the" is "da." So the sentence "I am going to the store" becomes "I am going ta da store."[9]

Crime and corruption are chronic concerns in Luzerne County. According to FBI crime reports, Wilkes-Barre has a violent crime rate that is 50 percent higher than the Pennsylvania average and 37 percent higher than the national average. And in Hazleton, between 2000 and 2014 there was a sixfold increase in robberies and a 70 percent increase in assaults.

People in Luzerne are cynical about corruption and think it's ingrained in the local culture, from the coal mining bosses of yesteryear to the Mafia, which established bases in Pittston and Hazleton from the 1950s into the 1990s. Congressman Dan Flood had to resign in disgrace in 1980 after being censured for bribery, while another area congressman, Joe McDade, was indicted in 1992, though he was acquitted. And in 2008, the so-called Kids for Cash scandal—in which two Luzerne judges and two businessmen were convicted of a kickback scheme to funnel arrested juveniles to a for-profit detention center in violation of their rights—resulted in thousands of convictions being tossed out, and provoked widespread outrage that lingers to this day.

Many Trump voters in the county say that this sordid history made them receptive to the frequent charges of corruption that Trump brought against Hillary Clinton in the campaign, over the use of her private email server and her alleged self-dealing through the Clinton Foundation.

But Tony Brooks thinks the locals overreact to corruption. "There's corruption everywhere, yet for some reason, in Wilkes-Barre, people think it only happened here," he says. "People feel they deserve to be downtrodden."

A 2011 Justice Department report said that there were at least twenty nationally known gangs active in half of the forty-two counties in eastern Pennsylvania, including Luzerne. It cited Hazleton as the strategic crossroads for drug distribution in the area because of its location at the intersection of Interstates 80 and 81.

"Crime is a big problem in this area, and we've seen a drastic increase in gang activity," says Stefanie Salavantis, the district attorney of Luzerne County. "In Wilkes-Barre, two factions of the Bloods shoot at each other in broad daylight right in front of police officers. I took office in 2012, when there were about five homicides a year in the county. In 2013, there were twenty-three. I'd say about 85 percent of those were related to drug abuse or addiction. We have people from New York and Philadelphia moving in here and transporting product."

Salavantis says that increasing the size of the police force to make cops more visible would be helpful, but the county can't afford it, or won't raise taxes to pay for it. She says she does a lot of talking to community groups to let them vent in what amounts to therapy sessions. She has also conducted about twenty community meetings educating people about their rights to carry a concealed weapon. She herself carries. "I grew up that way. My father and brothers were all hunters. I'm comfortable around guns."

But aging, lifelong residents of Luzerne are clearly uncomfortable with the increasingly frequent sounds of gunfire on their streets and the sight of drug dealers doing business openly and brazenly. Absentee landlords have let properties fall into disrepair, and sometimes the vacant houses are turned into drug dens or havens for squatters. Ambulances often roam the streets now, responding to calls about heroin overdoses.

In the enormous red expanse between the blue coasts, tens of thousands of working-class men are unemployed or on disability, and that has fueled a wave of despair in the form of the opioid epidemic. The problem is especially acute in mostly white, semirural areas like Luzerne County.

The county coroner, William Lisman, reported a record 154 fatal drug overdoses in 2017, primarily from heroin laced with fentanyl, which is cheaper to produce than heroin, and stronger. In a county of 320,000 people, that death rate is four times higher than New York City's.

Twenty years ago, Luzerne had fewer than twenty overdoses annually. In 2013 and 2014, there were sixty-seven overdoses, and in 2015, ninety-five—then a jump to 141 in 2016 and 154 in 2017.

Alarmed, Lisman went to one of the local newspapers to try and raise awareness about the issue. "I think a lot of people here are unhappy with their situation in life," he says. "When I was raised, you'd hitch up your pants and take care of your own problem. Now people don't seem as willing to deal with their own problems, and they want to escape to drugs."

The ages of people overdosing range from those in their twenties to those in their sixties, with the average age being thirty-eight, Lisman says. "Sometimes death comes as a relief to families. That's not right. Children are supposed to bury their parents, not vice versa. I've never experienced death as a feeling of relief. Now there is a sense of 'At least I can go to sleep and not worry about what they are doing anymore.'"

The death scenes can be gruesome. Deputy coroner Dan Hughes tells of one local woman who recently overdosed. When authorities responded to the call, they found an infant child eating Cheerios while lying on top of her mother, who had been dead for a few days.

Cathy Ryzner, a former heroin addict who now works to help others in recovery at Wyoming Valley Alcohol and Drug Services in Wilkes-Barre, worries that not enough is being done about the problem locally. "Addiction might be getting political attention, but it's all talk," she says. "Nothing is getting done. That's the way I feel. There is a stigma about heroin, especially in this area. Junkies are considered the scum of the earth. My mom always said we're good people with a bad disease. I grew up here. I love Luzerne County, but sometimes it's so backward. Heroin is all over the place, and there's a not-in-my-town attitude. They're trying to put a recovery center in the county but people are saying 'Not in my backyard.' People think there will be addicts on the street. There's no way this disease hasn't touched everyone or [at least] a family member. But it's a hidden disease."

Ryzner is a lifelong Democrat who voted for Donald Trump, and she knows plenty of others who did too. "Everyone got sick of the same old same old," she says. "People wanted to try someone who wasn't a politician. They wanted a change. I wanted a change, already!"

Indeed, there is some evidence that the opioid crisis had political repercussions in the 2016 election—in favor of Trump. He talked about the issue during the campaign, saying he would prosecute drug traffickers more aggressively and close shipping loopholes he said made it possible for China to bootleg fentanyl and ship it into the United States.

A research report from Penn State sociologist and demographer Shannon Monnat found that it was Trump who won counties in Pennsylvania and in the rest of the industrial Midwest, New England, and Appalachia, where both economic distress and mortality rates from drug overdoses were high.

"The promise of change was the common narrative,"

Monnat says. "Maybe people in Luzerne felt there was nothing to lose and did not want more of the same."

It's not as if addicts are a voting bloc, but their problems have had a profound ripple effect in the places they live. "Addiction has implications beyond the addicts themselves," Monnat says. "Symptoms of larger social and economic distress capture everyone who lives in these areas. Addicts' family members despair, employers find it hard to hire people who can pass a drug test, first responders and hospitals are overwhelmed by the problem. Everyone in the community is feeling this, and even if they're not addicted themselves, they probably know someone who is."

Monnat believes a key factor in people turning to drugs is the loss of dignity from not working or from being underemployed.

"We get a lot of our identity through our jobs," she says. "There's dignity in working, and if you are supporting your family, you're productive and giving back to society. If you can't, there's shame in that. Or you have to take lesser jobs that don't pay well—instead of building a car, you're working at Walmart. People in these types of places have been hearing the message from Democrats and the media that you have to go to college, and that's how you value work. That's been one of the frustrations in these places. Blue-collar workers get the message that their work doesn't matter and that they are replaceable. Trump exploited these feelings of anger, frustration, and despair."

Such feelings are contributing to higher death rates. In late 2015, two Princeton University professors published a study that found the national death rate among white men ages forty-five to fifty-four rose nearly 9 percent from 1999 to 2013, the most recent year for which data was available, while death rates for black and Hispanic men of the same age continued to decline. (Overall, the mortality rate in the United States has been declining 2 percent per year since the 1970s.) In a 2017 follow-up study, the professors, Anne Case and Angus Deaton, attributed the uptick to "deaths of despair" resulting from suicide, drugs, and alcohol due to rising unemployment and its attendant pain, distress, and social dysfunction.[10]

For all the problems that have seemed to overwhelm the people of Luzerne County—from the demise of its coal jobs to the loss of its manufacturing base to an economy struggling to adapt to the twenty-first century, with its rapid demographic changes and now a surging opioid epidemic—there is a resilience among those who remain and glimmers of hope for the region.

Early in 2018, it was announced that three major companies—Adidas, Patagonia, and Chewy.com, an online retailer of pet food—signed long-term leases for more than one million square feet of warehouse space being built on reclaimed mine lands in county industrial parks; these are deals that will create more than three thousand jobs. And a national real estate investor, NorthPoint Development, is building three additional facilities within the next five years that are expected to result in another fifteen hundred jobs.

In the summer of 2018, Luzerne hosted the Keystone State Games, Pennsylvania's largest amateur athletic festival and a highly competitive tourism event that brought in an estimated $10 million in revenue to the area.

Meanwhile, after years of running deficits, the county is getting its fiscal house in order. In 2017, Luzerne received only its second investment grade credit rating of the past thirty years. The county has paid off over $120 million in municipal debt in the past five years, passed a no-tax-increase budget for 2018, posted a surplus of more than $1 million in both 2016 and 2017, and added over $5 million worth of property to its tax rolls in 2017 and 2018.

And Wilkes-Barre is showing signs of revitalization and growth. The city's architectural gem, the county courthouse building on the Susquehanna River, is completing a $2 million restoration. Berkshire Hathaway Guard insurance recently made the city its international headquarters, bringing in hundreds of jobs. Apartment housing stock is on the rise due to demand from Berkshire Hathaway Guard, Pepperjam—a tech company founded in Wilkes-Barre—and students from area colleges like Wilkes University and King's College and the local campus of Penn State.

What's more, Hazleton is creating a fledgling Anglo-Hispanic culture, along with a revived downtown and a stable regional economy. It's enjoying a decline in crime under new police chief Jerry Speziale, who has increased the size of the force, implemented new technologies, and engaged the community through social media. A downtown renaissance in the city of Pittston, in the northeastern part of Luzerne, has also drawn statewide attention.

The county retains a strong civic and charitable culture. Local TV stations and newspapers provide frequent accounts of civic projects and charity organizations, including how Hazleton, for example, tackled its homelessness problem through a community-wide private partnership. Taverns and restaurants hold fund-raisers for needy families, and civic organizations like the Rotary Club still thrive.

"In many ways, Luzerne County is the crossroads for the changing socioeconomic and political dynamics of the country," says Charles McElwee. "The county never has, and will never become, a cultural cul-de-sac. And despite the challenges, it is difficult to measure the immense pride that still exists in Luzerne. It's a pride that germinated when the county was part of Pennsylvania's wilderness and extended its roots into coal and manufacturing. Today, the people here are doing their utmost—like others in thousands of communities across the country—to confront the challenges of a postindustrial economy undergoing rapid change."

THE CONGRESSMAN

Lou Barletta

BEFORE DONALD TRUMP ever talked tough on immigration and made it his signature issue in his run for president, there was Lou Barletta, who as the mayor of Hazleton in 2006 ignited a fierce debate about illegal immigrants that played out around the United States, and around the world.

Using state tax incentives, Barletta helped attract warehouse businesses to the city, and some five thousand jobs were created. The growing industrial base, along with the lure of cheap housing, helped draw thousands of Latinos to Hazleton—mostly Dominicans who had been living in New York or Philadelphia. In the 2000 census, just 4.9 percent of Hazleton's population identified as Hispanic. A decade later, that figure was 37 percent, and by 2016, it was 52 percent, so today Hazleton has a Hispanic majority, like the nearby cities of Reading and Allentown, south of Luzerne County in eastern Pennsylvania.

As the Hispanics began arriving in earnest around 2000, some of Hazleton's white old guard grew alarmed. Immigrants are welcome, they would invariably say, but they should arrive the way their grandparents did: legally, through places like Ellis Island. A different language was now being spoken, violent crime increased, a cultural chasm developed, and white flight ensued. Then, in May 2006, after a white Hazleton man was shot in the head and killed, and two Dominican illegal immigrants were arrested for the shooting, Barletta decided that he had seen enough and decided to take action.

At a raucous city council meeting packed with opposing white and Latino factions, the mayor, wearing a bulletproof vest, pushed through the Illegal Immigration Relief Act, which imposed a $1,000-per-day fine on any landlord who rented to an illegal immigrant, and revoked for five years the business license of any employer who hired one. The legislation also made English the official language of Hazleton, and forbade city employees to translate documents into any other language without permission. After the vote, some whites in the audience taunted the Hispanics in the crowd by singing the chorus of "Hit the Road, Jack." A Latino leader fretted that Hazleton was turning into a "Nazi city."

Barletta added fuel to the fire, telling the *Washington Post* at the time that he wanted "to make Hazleton the toughest place on illegal immigrants in America...I will get rid of the illegal people. It's this simple: they must leave."

He said the illegal immigrants were overwhelming his city, draining its resources, and hurting residents' quality of life. Serious crime had doubled in the past two years; Hazleton's thirty-one-man police force was not equipped to deal with that increase, and had blown through its overtime budget. In the schools, the cost of teaching English as a second language had gone from $500 a year to more than $875,000 annually.

The story exploded. In addition to speaking with national newspapers, Barletta did a star turn on *60 Minutes,* and was interviewed by German, Italian, and Japanese television as well. Other cities in the United States took note and adopted Hazleton's tough immigration law verbatim.

But then prosecutors dropped the murder charges against the two Dominicans, citing insufficient evidence, and deported them instead. Meanwhile, the American Civil Liberties Union and the Puerto Rican Legal Defense and Education Fund sued to block the ordinance. A federal judge in Scranton ruled against Barletta and the city of Hazleton, saying they had usurped the authority of the federal government, which regulates immigration, and violated the due process rights of landlords, employers, and illegal immigrants themselves.

Barletta promised an appeal, vowing to take his fight to the U.S. Supreme Court, if necessary. "I will not sit back because the federal government has refused to do its job," he said at a news conference on the steps of city hall. The spectacle recalled Governor George Wallace's famed Stand in the Schoolhouse Door in 1963, when he temporarily blocked a Justice Department official from entering the University of Alabama to enforce an integration order.

When the federal Third Circuit Court of Appeals upheld the district court's ruling against the city, Barletta ordered, as he had pledged, an appeal to the Supreme Court. The high court initially gave Barletta reason for hope, ordering the

Third Circuit to reconsider its decision, based on a ruling in Arizona that had upheld a law similar to Hazleton's. But when the Third Circuit stood by its decision, and the Supreme Court declined further involvement, the legal battle was over.

In the end, Hazleton was ordered to pay nearly $1.4 million in legal fees and court costs, but by then, the ambitious Barletta had already ridden the hullabaloo over the case to a seat in Congress, defeating the twenty-five-year Democratic incumbent, Paul Kanjorski, on his third attempt.

During the uproar over his Illegal Immigration Relief Act, Barletta's critics assailed him as a bigoted opportunist, and when Hazleton lost the lawsuit and had to shell out the $1.4 million in taxpayer funds, he was called fiscally irresponsible as well. But he denied any racist intent and defended the ordinance as having been well worth the fight.

"When we first passed the ordinance, we literally saw people leaving in the middle of the night," Barletta says today. "There was a restraining order put on us so we never got to enforce it. The media keeps confusing legal immigrants, who I'm all for, with illegals, even though I've been so careful to point out we're talking about *illegal* immigrants. They leave the word 'illegal' out. So, I started using 'illegal alien,' even though I don't like the term, so they couldn't change my meaning.

"The other point, which they never report, is that Hazleton's Hispanic population has grown every year since the ordinance passed. Why come to Hazleton if you don't feel welcome? The real story is that Hazleton *does* accept immigrants. That never gets reported. Reporters talk to the same people who are against it and get the same answers. So, the idea that because I stood up on illegal immigration I'm somehow anti-immigrant is fiction made up by the media, because that's what they believe."

Barletta is the youngest of four boys born to Rocco and Angeline Barletta. Lou was born and raised in Hazleton, where everyone lived near their churches. There was the Irish church, the Italian church, the Slovak church, and so on. That's how neighborhoods were organized at the time.

Rocco, who had six brothers and two sisters, dropped out of school after the eighth grade and went to work with his father picking coal. Later, the family started a sand and gravel business and opened a grocery store. Then it was an asphalt, paving, and road-building business. Rocco also built an amusement park in honor of his mother, Angela, called Angela Park, in Drums, just north of Hazleton.

It seemed as though everyone Lou knew worked at the park. He had more than twenty male cousins, and three who were his age were his best friends. Everyone in the extended family had to work, so they all worked in the family businesses.

"They'd take us out of school for special days down at the amusement park," Barletta remembers. "We'd fill sodas, make pizza boxes, and work at the mini golf course. Eventually, I ran one of the rides in the park. Then, when I was fourteen or fifteen, I moved over to the family construction company to work. I always believed that's where my life was going to be, because that's what my cousins and brothers all did."

Lou, his brothers, and his cousins would go to school, and afterward, they'd walk over to the family construction

company, where, at the end of the day, his dad and his six uncles and their sons would all hang out.

"The language of the construction company was pretty col-
orful. They yelled a lot, and my dad and his brothers fought
a lot. That's where the real education came. They were a
tough Italian family. They could fight—over anything that
happened about construction, who should be hitting third for
the Yankees, or anything. They fought like hell. It was like a
movie. But God forbid someone said anything negative about
the others: they wouldn't leave the office in one piece. It was
a tight family. Very tight. The thing they taught us: you work,
you do anything you were told to do, and you don't complain
about it. I guess it toughened you up.

"No one in my immediate family went to college. I was
the first, though to be honest, I didn't care very much for it.
I wanted to play baseball. I wanted to play center field for the
New York Yankees."

Once he realized that wasn't going to happen, Barletta
enrolled in nearby Bloomsburg State College and studied ele-
mentary education. There he met and married his wife, Mary
Grace, while still in college. Mary Grace was Irish, which to
Lou's mother made theirs a "mixed marriage." Lou and Mary
Grace have been married for more than forty years and have
four daughters and eight grandchildren.

In his third year at Bloomsburg, his baseball dream flickered
again when he got a letter from the Cincinnati Reds inviting
him to a tryout.

"I had to tell my father I might quit school. He was a
strong, imposing man. But he said, 'Don't be afraid. If there's
something you want to do in life, do it.' So I quit school, went

to Florida, and enrolled in Bucky Dent's baseball school to practice up. Then I tried out. The Reds claimed I couldn't hit a curve. But I was fast. I could go from home to first in 3.7 seconds. They suggested I try out for Toronto or Seattle as a walk-on. But I never played baseball again, until I got to Congress."

Barletta returned to the family construction company, upset with himself because it seemed as if he'd failed, and not just at baseball—he hadn't graduated from college either. But now he couldn't go back to school because he was married and had two children to support.

One day, he got a card in the mail advertising a kit that taught people how to stripe their own parking lot. "I told my wife, 'I got a great idea: we're going to start a line painting business.' She should have left me that day . . .

"I quit my job, sent away for the kit for twenty-nine ninety-five, and got a case of aerosol to start. I walked into a local bank and walked out with a twenty-five-hundred-dollar line of credit. I was able to buy a little machine, then a truck, then another truck, and in five years, our company, the Interstate Road Marking Corporation, grew to be the largest in the state of Pennsylvania and the sixth largest in the country. It literally was like an American dream come true."

Then Barletta decided to get involved in local politics. He'd come from a Democratic family and his dad had once been chairman of the Hazleton City Democrats, but the family later became Republicans, and Lou followed suit, joining the GOP in 1988, when he was thirty-two. "I was always a Reagan Democrat," he says. "My wife's uncle was involved with the Hazleton City Republican Party. He asked me to switch parties during the primary to help a Republican candidate for mayor in the city. So I did, to help him out, but I liked President Reagan and his policies. I never switched back."

Spurring Barletta's entry into politics had been a drumbeat of negative headlines in the 1990s about Hazleton that unnerved him. There seemed to be a lot of craziness afoot: a city councilman was beaten up by the city highway foreman, the administration wasn't sharing enough information with the public, city council meetings were like a circus. Barletta felt that Hazleton was getting a bad image and wondered why the city couldn't be run like a business. So he ran for the council in 1996 and lost. He ran again in 1998 and won, and then ran for mayor in 2000 and was elected. Being mayor was a full-time job, so he sold his line painting business.

Barletta found that the city was bankrupt and had a $1.2 million shortfall on a $7 million budget. There were illegal contracts with the labor unions because the previous mayor had negotiated the contracts without council approval.

"In two years we were able to turn that $1.2 million deficit into a half-million-dollar surplus," says Barletta. "Thirty percent of downtown stores were occupied when I first started as mayor. When I left, it was ninety percent. I thought we needed to get people back into downtown. How are you going to start a business if there are no people there?" When he ran for reelection, he won by a four-to-one margin and by 90 percent on his third campaign for mayor. By this time, the Latino population had started to grow and the illegal immigration issue had emerged.

Barletta thought the best way to get people downtown was to build a neighborhood. So he quietly had the city begin to acquire property in a three-block area around Hazleton's Pine Street Playground.

"We went door-to-door—this was mainly a Latino neighborhood now—and I asked, 'If I built a playground, what kind of playground would you want?' They wanted a soccer field. So, we built a soccer field with artificial turf that could be flooded in the winter for skating. I wanted to make sure the housing was affordable. After we acquired enough properties, we made the announcement.

"This was right in the center of the city of Hazleton, near abandoned warehouses and neglected properties. It was a high-crime and very blighted area in town. I used Community Development Block Grants. People thought I was crazy and wanted to throw me out of town. They asked why was I doing this in a bad area. But we sold every home, and there was a waiting list to get in. We won awards. The houses were about a hundred and twenty-five thousand dollars. But we could write down some of the costs to ninety thousand. I thought people would take better care of their houses if they owned them, rather than rented, and had some skin in the game. That began the comeback of downtown. Our population in Hazleton grew by fifty percent from 2000 to 2005, but our tax revenue stayed the same. I realized we had an illegal immigration problem. Here was a city that was crawling back, good things were happening. But the city was fifty percent bigger, and we didn't have the money for services."

One day in 2001, Barletta was called to look at an apartment where someone had reported that there were problems. He saw nine mattresses on the floor, and there were cockroaches everywhere. All nine men were in the country illegally.

"We called INS—it wasn't ICE yet. They said, 'Let them go. Tell them to move on.' I didn't understand that.

"We began seeing more violent crime. We found a pattern that there were more and more illegal immigrants involved in crime. The media twists that to say *only* illegal immigrants are committing crimes. That's not true."

Barletta began getting more pressure from white Hazleton residents to do something about illegal immigration. One day in 2004, he arrived at work to find an elderly woman waiting for him in his city hall parking space. "She said, 'You'd better do something, buster. I can't even sit on my own porch. I've become a prisoner in my own home.'

"It was a combination of crimes happening and my wanting to do something. The feds weren't helping at all. I thought stopping the illegals wasn't going to solve all crimes, but it was going to do something. It certainly was going to plug holes, because the ship was sinking fast and I was trying to bail water out as fast as I could."

Barletta says the 2006 murder of a Hazleton man for which the two Dominican illegal immigrants were arrested was "the final straw." That's when he pushed through the city council his Illegal Immigration Relief Act, which imposed tough fines on landlords renting to illegals and revoked the business licenses of any companies that hired them.

"People were asking me to do something, and I did. Naturally the media swarmed into town, and I just spoke honestly. I didn't think I did anything wrong. But when the media came in and accused me of being racist, it felt like I did something wrong. The term I used was, 'Illegal is illegal.' That summed it up."

That phrase became Barletta's mantra. Confronted with any skeptical question by the press or anyone else, he would just repeat, "Illegal is illegal."

The turmoil that followed—national and international press coverage, the Dominican suspects of the murder in Hazleton being released for lack of evidence, the city being sued for discrimination and ultimately losing an expensive court battle, and considerable white flight—has left wounds that are still healing.

"It was a very sad time," recalls Krista Schneider, executive director of the Downtown Hazleton Alliance for Progress, a group working to promote Hispanic integration into the city. "The entire Hispanic community was being viewed as unwelcome, and they continue to feel unwelcome. It was a big divide."

Another important organization working to help Hispanics adapt is the Hazleton Integration Project, which runs English as a second language classes for the Hispanic community and Spanish classes for whites, as well as sports, drama, and dance programs—primarily for schoolchildren.

The group was founded by Bob Curry and his wife, Elaine, in 2013, and it received significant funding from Elaine's cousin, Chicago Cubs manager and Hazleton native Joe Maddon.

"When we opened our doors, we got some criticism," Curry says. "There were negative comments. The theme was, this was just another giveaway for Hispanics, we shouldn't be supporting these newcomers, we should make it all white— stuff we did not pay attention to. There was misunderstanding and miscommunication and there was palpable tension. We had a true white-versus-Hispanic rift through the city at that time. I think people questioned whether people they knew were here legally. But over time, what happened was, a sense of normalcy started to return as people realized that those they were working with in the industrial parks around Hazleton were kind of like they were. Hispanic kids started playing ball with white kids in Little League. Now most of the comments we get are, 'Hey, you guys are doing a great job.' We're just sticking to the mission: we love the kids, trying to give them the same opportunity as everyone else. We work with the school district and universities. We feed kids after school, provide food to families. We have after-school programs.

"When Trump won, I think people were stunned, and there was disbelief from the newcomers who didn't think Trump would win. And there was a sense of fear and displacement again. Some of that fear has begun to lessen, but the jury is still out. They wonder, *What is he going to do?* As far as the Caucasians go, they think someone is finally listening to them. That 'America First' phrase in some ways has been interpreted as '*white* Americans first.' Whether that comes to pass, we'll see."

And how has Lou Barletta responded to the Hazleton Integration Project? "Lou has been—and this surprises people—very supportive of what we do," Curry says. "He's been here ten or twelve times. We don't agree with Congressman Barletta on a lot of things. He knows that. We know that. But it doesn't do us any good to scream about it. We keep the dialogue open. We try and impress upon him what our view is, and he has been respectful of our position."

Barletta says it should be no surprise that he supports the

group. "I think it's a good program. I've been close friends with Joe Maddon. Anytime you can help children, whether it's learning English or assimilating, that's good." He stresses that he supports continued *legal* immigration to Hazleton and Luzerne County. "Of course I do. It's America, and we're a country of immigrants."

Barletta is building tentative bridges to groups like the Hazleton Integration Project and to the larger Hispanic community, but his base remains the white majority of Luzerne County and northeast Pennsylvania who strongly oppose illegal immigration. They are less than thrilled about legal immigration too, to the extent that it results in changing the demographics of their communities and creates a cultural dissonance. And they still appreciate the hard line Barletta took as mayor of Hazleton in 2006, and the way he spoke bluntly about a hot-button issue of vital importance to them.

"What Lou did was give people permission to say what they feel," says Eddie Pashinski, the Democratic state representative for Luzerne County, not unadmiringly. Trump, of course, would do the same thing when he ran for president ten years later, giving voice to his supporters not just on illegal immigration, but on a variety of other issues as well.

"I was walking a fine line," Barletta says about giving voice to others. "You don't want to be accused of being a racist. A lot of these conversations were probably held behind closed doors. I said what I felt. Whether that gave cover to others who felt the same way—it probably did."

Ten years after the Hazleton uproar, when Donald Trump emerged as the leading contender for the Republican presidential nomination, Barletta knew he had found a kindred spirit on the illegal immigration issue. He became one of the first members of Congress to endorse Trump's candidacy.

"Ten years after Hazleton, Trump said, 'We're going to build a wall,' and that hit the nail on the head," Barletta says. "They called him racist, and it reminded me of what they had called me ten years ago. I didn't know what I did wrong. I just said 'Illegal is illegal.' I didn't understand why people were objecting.

"Now here was a candidate who was openly talking about the problem, and I didn't remember a president talking that way. He was saying what I was thinking, and what others were thinking. He talked about securing the borders and defending the laws, and I was impressed that he didn't back down."

TRUMP MEN

Vito DeLuca

VITO

Vito DeLuca, fifty, is a self-described Reagan Democrat with his own law practice outside Wilkes-Barre.

Back when he first became eligible to vote, Vito wanted to register as a Republican, but he said his father, Joseph DeLuca, a retired plasterer and a staunch Democrat, refused to allow it and made him sign up as a Democrat.

In 2016, Vito—ever respectful of his dad—dared not even tell him that he was voting for Donald Trump, since Joe was a Hillary Clinton supporter who thought Trump was crude and unqualified. But for Vito, Hillary was not an option, and Trump was intriguing.

"I'm first-generation college," Vito says. "I was getting

tired of the traditional political message. I believed Hillary Clinton to be someone who was not trustworthy. I believed that in her years and years of public service, she saw to it that she and her husband were always taken care of, financially. Her message was the same message that had been repeated by politicians for years and years, and they did nothing. I had read Trump's *Art of the Deal* when I was much younger. He obviously wasn't a politician, but he had business acumen. My whole thing was, it was time to think outside the box, get a nonpolitician, give him a shot and see what he could do."

That said, Vito realized he was voting for the most unusual candidate in his lifetime, and he held his breath a bit. "I remember wondering when I was voting for Trump if I was going to cast a vote for Armageddon. It was tongue-in-cheek, because I had confidence that there are checks and balances in terms of what he can execute. I can't imagine that in cartoon fashion he could be provoked to order a nuclear strike."

The oldest of Joe and Janice DeLuca's three sons, Vito grew up in Newport Township, a community of about five thousand people, twelve miles southwest of Wilkes-Barre.

Janice was a stay-at-home mom until Vito was in high school; then she went to work for a local bank, as a secretary. As a kid, Vito would often go out and work with his dad. "I'd mix plaster and bust out a sidewalk with him. My dad was an extremely hard worker. He'd work for friends or whoever. He'd install Sheetrock and do carpentry too. He worked for a nonunion ceiling company for fifteen years. The company bid on some prevailing wage jobs. He'd work out of the union hall sometimes too, but there weren't enough of those jobs to go around."

Joe DeLuca's father, Vito, for whom young Vito was named, was a lifelong union laborer who died of prostate cancer just after he turned sixty. Joe was also a civic leader; he served as a commissioner in Newport Township for over twenty years. He was active in local Democratic politics and was someone county officials relied on to work for them at the polls.

Young Vito would frequently discuss politics with his father and grandfather, who was also a loyal Democrat. "I used to get into arguments with my grandfather about Reagan versus Jimmy Carter. I don't know if I've ever been philosophically in line with the Democrats at the presidential level. I always vote the candidate, not the party."

Joe DeLuca, seventy-one, says he's surprised that Vito felt he might get in trouble with him for voting for Trump.

"He's not going to get in trouble with me. He does what he wants. He's his own man. He would have been a Republican from the get-go if I wasn't so in deep to the Democrats. He registered as a Democrat out of the goodness of his heart for me. But it is what it is. If he wants to be a Republican, that's his business. I've been a Democrat from day one. I thought they were for the average people, and Republicans for the rich. That's my view."

But Joe DeLuca admits to not being happy with Hillary as a candidate, and he understands how people could have been attracted to Trump.

"I was surprised he won as big as he did in Luzerne County, because in Newport Township, the Republicans could hold a convention in a phone booth. We're three to one Democrats, but people are fed up with the government and they wanted a change."

The DeLuca family celebrated its Italian heritage.

"I always identified as an Italian American as a young kid," Vito says. "I mean, with a name like Vito it's hard not to. My father and grandfather were very proud of it. We had Italian and Easter traditions. My *nonna* was a typical Italian grandmother who worked in a sewing factory."

Joe DeLuca is a devout Catholic, but Vito resisted following suit.

"I was raised Catholic, but I've grown cynical about much of the Catholic religion. I began questioning it when I was very young. I was an altar boy, and first child lector. My mom, who is of German descent, was Protestant, but she converted to Catholicism before marrying my dad. Still, I really started questioning everything early on. I thought it was sexist, putting men above women, and I didn't like the Catholic view of homosexuality, or reconciling an all-good God with original sin. I would debate with my mom, who was trying to keep us good Catholics . . . I could see she was somewhat half-hearted about it, not having been born into Catholicism. My dad would keep us in the fold to the extent he would be sure to get our butts out of bed and into church. But I would not debate my dad about the church. He taught me how to be a man, about honesty and the value of hard work and treating others how you would like to be treated. We'd lift weights together. My mom took on the role of the intellectual aide. My dad would push me in a different way, physically, and he taught me skills."

Having graduated from high school in 1986, Vito was too

young to have voted for Ronald Reagan, though he wishes he could have.

"When I was eighteen, I was a Reaganite. That was the time of the movies *Wall Street* and *The Secret of My Success*. And Trump with his book *Art of the Deal*. So, as a kid going to school in finance and economics, and looking at law school, I think I identified with Republican principles and supply-side economics, even though I didn't fully understand what that was at the time."

He initially registered as a Republican, but after his horrified father insisted that he become a Democrat, Vito obeyed, and says today he could see merit in the move. "This was part of the culture in our area. If you wanted to get anywhere, you had to be a Democrat."

After going to King's College in Wilkes-Barre and the University of Pittsburgh School of Law, Vito returned home, clerked for two local judges, and took a job working for the Luzerne County public defender's office part-time. "Being a Democrat was key. The political side was important."

In 1993, Vito started his own law practice, specializing in criminal defense work. At the same time, with a goal of running for office someday, he further immersed himself in local politics by taking a job as an assistant solicitor, helping to represent Luzerne County in various legal claims brought against it.

In 2007, at age thirty-eight, Vito made his first bid for public office by running for district attorney of Luzerne. But he got a rude awakening and lost badly in the Democratic primary to a woman who had been serving as the first assistant DA, and who went on to win the general election.

Shortly thereafter, in 2008, Vito was appointed chief solicitor by the Luzerne County commissioners, who valued his experience as an assistant solicitor. The job paid $50,000 a year, plus benefits, but there were no strict rules about whether it had to be full-time, so he could still maintain his law practice.

No sooner did he take the chief solicitor job than the Kids for Cash scandal erupted, resulting in hundreds of convictions being tossed out, generating national publicity and shame for the county.

Vito had hoped that being chief solicitor would help him earn name recognition in the county and be an asset in running for office, but it probably had the opposite effect, because people were in a mood to punish all public officials. "Even though I was not there when the crimes were committed, the public perception was to 'throw 'em all out.'"

Vito served as chief solicitor from 2008 to 2012. During that period, which saw the public condemnation of the Kids for Cash crew, several row officers (a largely Pennsylvanian term referring to elected officials like the sheriff, court clerk, and registrar of deeds) were caught up in wrongdoing of one sort or another and "dropping like flies, one by one," Vito recalls. "So the cushy solicitor's job turned into a twenty-four-hour nightmare. It was like sweeping a dirt floor. Every time you thought you were getting somewhere, you'd find three other things."

The voters had had enough, and in 2010, following the recommendation of a government study commission, they approved a new home rule charter that made sweeping changes to county government. These included a new governing structure of eleven county commissioners, instead of three, who appointed a county manager.

Vito made two other bids for elected office—a campaign for a local judgeship, in 2011, and a second race for DA, in 2015—both of which he lost decisively. "I think I had a bloated view of what my service to the county had been, and I think that hurt me more than helped me," he says today. "I also think I had an inflated view of my name recognition."

The approval of a home rule charter weakened the Democratic Party in Luzerne County. "Before home rule," Vito says, "the Democrats had a two-to-one advantage in party registration. Every row officer was a Democrat and had his own power base... Whenever outside candidates came to town, they didn't have to go to every barbecue: they just went to these row officers, who had their own base. If you look at the government study commission, it emasculated the Democratic Party."

Vito noted an increased cynicism among voters about government officials—an assumption that many, or most, were corrupt. After his stint as chief solicitor, he assembled a network of part-time solicitor jobs representing various municipalities and school districts in the county. "In one of the school districts, a man in the neighborhood, rather than congratulate me for taking the new position, simply noted that we were building a new school, and he said all the school board members and the solicitor would of course get a cut of the new school funds. That to me was a clear indication that people believed unethical dealings were a way of doing business in officialdom for years, and that there was a culture of corruption."

So when Donald Trump regularly accused Hillary Clinton of corruption during the campaign, many Luzerne voters related to the message.

"I have absolutely no doubt about that," Vito says. "Don't forget, I was right there in county government when the corruption and arrests were occurring... There were many angry people. Plus, a good part of Trump's vote was because Clinton couldn't come in and mobilize the traditional Democratic organization. It was completely gone."

Vito's first presidential vote had been for George H. W. Bush. He voted against Bill Clinton twice, for George W. Bush twice, and for John McCain over Barack Obama in 2008, but he voted for Obama in 2012. "I was not moved at all by Mitt Romney," Vito explains. "Obama always reminded me of Jimmy Carter, a guy who I thought had a kind soul, who was more trustworthy than most politicians, but was generally not effective as a president. I think my vote for Obama was rewarding him for being a good guy, and I didn't think Romney was good enough—certainly not the object of change that would motivate me."

Trump was an object of change, all right, but he seemed a wild card. "During the campaign, I wasn't happy with a lot of Trump's knee-jerk responses to critics; that seemed to lack discipline. But to me, Hillary wasn't an option. My two options were not to vote or vote for Trump.

"My hope was Trump was going to make change. He couldn't make change without being elected. I'd hoped after he won the nomination that he would act more presidential. It was extremely interesting to me that I believed the media were beating the hell out of him on a number of issues—any one of which would have sunk any other candidate. But because the media was so insistent on Trump not winning, all they did was turn his mini controversies into white noise. If anything, his name just got out there more and more.

"Trump supporters looked at all this and concluded he was the underdog. We thought, *I'm not that dumb. I'm not going to let the media sway me.* True, Trump said what he said. But the media, if their goal was to marginalize him, failed miserably. They stayed on him, and admittedly, he was not acting presidential, but did that always deserve a full news day?"

Vito says he listens to Fox News on satellite radio. Then he'll put on CNN, but that will agitate him, and he goes back to Fox. "It's tough to get objective, nonbiased reporting these days...I had MSN.com as my Web page and I just changed it because every single article seems to be about what a bad man our president is. My view is, when you have a president, you root for them—you don't do everything you can to undermine them. Once a president is elected, I support them. During Bill Clinton's eight years, I rooted for him because he was the president, even though I didn't vote for him. Now the Trump haters won't let it go, already! Their candidate lost the election. So, rally behind the guy who won, and wait for next campaign season before you go out and bash the guy. I don't see Trump getting the same respect as there has been for past presidents."

Overall, Vito concluded that Trump was perhaps a unique change agent who deserved a chance to be president, despite the fact that Vito disagreed with him on issues like the border wall and the environment, and didn't like his divisive, often unpresidential style.

Vito thinks it's too early in Trump's term to make definitive judgments. "I was out at a local bar the other night with a lot of union friends. I was asking them why they voted for Trump and what he's accomplished... Their response, and I think mine as well, is that the reasons people went for Trump was not a Democrat-Republican thing: it was an insider-outsider thing. I had expectations he was going to have problems with Congress. I don't think the establishment Republicans bought into the concept of an outsider like Trump coming in and draining the swamp.

"I think the economic climate is better off than it was a year ago, but we're worse off in some respects too, like the environment. And I'm concerned with how his rhetoric is affecting race relations. I think a side effect of his in-your-face style is that he says many things that can be misconstrued or misinterpreted."

While Trump's statements on race and women have concerned Vito, he's giving him the benefit of the doubt.

"Sure, there were a number of different stories that came out that gave me pause about his character. And despite my desire to have someone like him be able to effect change, I wondered, was this someone that I would be proud to have voted for? But when I saw some of his responses to whether he was racist or sexist—this was a guy who'd had women in different levels of management... I really believed he was someone who would see the value of people beyond race, creed, and color and make the choice on people who would make him look best."

Vito concedes that racism may have played a role in Trump's election. "It may have played a part. Some of his actions might have been misconstrued and used as a rallying cry. The 'Build the wall' part, for example. These immigrants are people, most of them, who are coming here to make a better life for themselves. I was a little concerned about some of his statements causing a divide. Because I don't believe he's a racist. But it's unfortunate how he reacts to some things without seeming to think it through, as to whether it has consequences, in terms of people's perceptions."

Vito likes Trump's record as a businessman, and the fact that "he did not make it on 'the government suck,' as they say around here," whereas he thinks Hillary did. "I have some questions about the Clinton Foundation, and whether government influence was used to raise money for that."

On illegal immigration, Vito says he supports border security, but thinks a wall is unnecessary. "I never took President Trump's campaign promises regarding construction of a wall literally, and I'm concerned with the tension the wall issue may be creating within the Latino community."

On Trump's divisive rhetoric, Vito resigned himself to the idea that it was largely a device Trump was using to get elected, and that in the White House he would reach out and try to unify the country more. "On election night I thought he was conciliatory and gracious and very presidential. So when I went to sleep that night, I said, 'You know what? I did the right thing.'"

After getting drubbed in his second run for district attorney, in 2015, despite twenty-five years of experience as a lawyer and serving in government, Vito decided his career was at a crossroads.

"I believed there was more that I had to offer... When I was a kid, it was either be a lawyer or a doctor. But I've been a lawyer now for twenty-five years. I've done homicides, drug cases, probably eighty jury trials, divorce and custody cases—you name it. But after I lost the DA election, it just hit me that I might contribute in a different way."

So Vito has gone back to a community college and taken a range of premed courses, including chemistry, biochemistry, anatomy, physiology, pharmacology, and radiology. He'd always enjoyed science and had an aptitude for it, having rung up a 3.9 grade point average in his college science work.

Now he's studying for the AMCAS test, the all-important standardized exam required by medical schools and administered by the American Medical College Application Service.

Most of his law practice now is municipal and his hours are flexible, affording him time to take his premed classes.

At age fifty, Vito realizes it's late to be changing careers but says, "You only live once, and my age is what it is. I'm thankful for the opportunity to further my education. In the beginning, it was so daunting. So I decided to take baby steps. Four credits at a time."

His wife, Maria, and their three sons are all supportive. Another motivating factor for Vito was the fact that his middle son was enrolled in a premed program at Syracuse University.

"I was taking organic chem as he was taking general chemistry. My middle son was the one I was worried about not having enough in common with. So we bonded further about med school. He wouldn't go to tutors—he'd call me. Still to this day he does. He'd text me questions during the day, and say he'd call me at night. I'd spend hours getting the answer and learning how to convey it to him. He doesn't know it took me that long to prepare.

"So even if I don't do well enough on the AMCAS to go to med school, learning about the absolute magic that is organic chemistry, learning how you breathe and eat, and building the relationship with my middle son has been a fabulous process. So I'm thankful for this experience no matter how it turns out."

Ed Harry

ED

Ed Harry, seventy-two, is a veteran of the war in Vietnam, where he served in an Air Force unit that was attached to the National Security Agency.

The son of a coal miner, Ed grew up in Luzerne County, worked as a labor organizer, immersed himself in Democratic politics, and rose to become president of the Wilkes-Barre Labor Council.

But when his union endorsed Hillary Clinton before the Pennsylvania primary in 2016, Ed resigned—and announced that he was voting for Donald Trump.

"I was a Democrat for fifty-two years of my life," he says.

"My whole voting life. I was even an elected delegate for Bill Clinton in 1992. Then NAFTA and GATT happened and I became disillusioned. There was a new globalization in America and I was looking for an alternative. The Democrats have been slipping away from the people for a long time. The six top richest people in the country now are Democrats, so they have become the mean and nasty people. We lost our party. It got taken away from us."

Not that he saw the Republican Party as the party of the people either. He simply came to conclude that both parties were corrupt.

But Hillary Clinton was especially anathema to Ed. "She should be in jail over Benghazi and the Clinton Foundation. She did not go out and meet people like me. She just wanted big money from Wall Street. She took people for granted, and we got fed up with all that. We think there are two sets of standards: one for the politicians and one for the rest of us."

Trump was an outsider but initially hard for Ed to take seriously. "At first I sort of laughed at Trump. I didn't think he was credible, but the more I listened to him and watched him in action, [the more I saw that] he was an advocate for things I believed in, like getting rid of TPP [the Trans-Pacific Partnership]. No more trade agreements. And something had to be done with immigration."

Trump's financing of his own campaign also appealed to Ed because it meant he was independent. "That would have played good for me no matter who it was. I think most of the people in Washington are blackmailed because they've been compromised by money and political contributions."

And he liked the way Trump talked, especially without

observing the traditional niceties. "Trump talks like you and I talk. He calls it the way it is. The political correctness today is so over the top. I don't like people telling me what to think, or how I should think... Come on, give me a break! I'm not a two-year-old who can't think for himself. Don't call me out and tell me I'm stupid because I don't think the way the ultraliberals do.

"And why are the Russians the bad guys? You've got the Chinese and the North Koreans practicing slave labor. Russian spying is no big thing. It's been going on for years."

Ed and his younger sister grew up in Plymouth, a borough in the center of Luzerne County just west of Wilkes-Barre, and he still lives in the house his family has occupied since 1949.

His mom worked in the local dress factories, where she was active in her union and led the occasional strike. Ed thinks that's what sparked his interest in the labor movement.

His dad, the coal miner, was five eight and weighed about 270 pounds. He was illiterate, which Ed didn't know at the time. It seemed as though his father had always worked in the mines. He drank beer. He volunteered for his fire company, which was a social club for a lot of the local men.

One day, when Ed was a senior in high school, his dad came home from work, took a water glass, filled it up with whiskey, and drank it. Then he poured himself another glass, filling it about halfway this time. Then he started crying. The roof had caved in on his mine shaft that day. He and his friends made it out, but he swore he'd never go back in the mines again, and now he was worried about how he'd support his family.

"That was very traumatic for him—and for me, needless

to say," says Ed, a stocky man with a mustache and white hair that is usually covered with a ski cap in winter and a Penn State ball cap in summer. He favors sweatshirts, and often has a toothpick dangling from his mouth.

The coal industry was dying at the time his dad quit the mines, so Ed asked an older friend who was a leading local Democrat to help his father get a job working as a laborer for the Pennsylvania Department of Transportation, or PennDOT, as it is known locally. It was a patronage job. Ed's whole family was Republican, but he was the first to register as a Democrat because all his friends were Democrats. There was little job security at PennDOT. None of the jobs were unionized, and if you weren't civil service, you usually got fired when the governorship changed.

Ed's dad lived until he was eighty, and his mom, an asthmatic, until she was seventy-five. Ed thinks the most his family ever made was $5,000 a year.

"We were all so poor, I didn't know what the hell the middle class was. I didn't know how bad my parents had it until I graduated high school. But no one had their doors locked. Me and my friends used to eat at each other's houses. I grew up in an area where there were about eighteen or nineteen guys my own age. We played sports all day. If we weren't in school, we were out in the summer playing ball. In the winter, we played basketball in the snow."

Ed graduated from Plymouth High School in 1964 and, after working for a year, entered Mansfield State College, up on the New York line. He stayed for a semester and then quit. He didn't know what he wanted to do, and his parents couldn't afford the tuition anyway.

Then he got drafted. He joined the Air Force in April 1966. Why the Air Force? He figured the Marines and the Army drew the heaviest duty, and he had liked the Air Force recruiters when they came to Plymouth High.

Ed became a radio intercept analyst, tasked with monitoring, collecting, and interpreting military voice and electronic signals from countries of interest—and also from American pilots, to make sure they were on the straight and narrow. He was assigned to the Air Force Security Service, which was essentially an offshoot of the NSA. He left for Southeast Asia in January 1968 and was based in Thailand, but he made frequent forays into Da Nang and into Tan Son Nhut Air Base in Vietnam. Thai headquarters was the Nakhon Phanom Royal Thai Air Force Base, known as NKP, which was used by the United States in its fight against North Vietnam and the Pathet Lao communist guerrillas in Laos from 1961 to 1975. The CIA's Air America was also based at NKP.

"We'd tap into conversations of people who worked there to monitor if what they were talking about was legit," Ed says. "In Vietnam, we'd go to Tan Son Nhut or Da Nang and monitor every communication that took place between the pilots and the towers. We wanted to make sure pilots did not give their coordinates, so the enemy wouldn't know where they were. We also monitored American conversations, including the Air America pilots.

"I was one of the guys sent into Laos to work with the CIA, but soon rotated back. We broke the war effort in Laos. We froze it. Americans weren't supposed to be there and we blew the whistle on illegal U.S. ops there. But they never shut it down. They just did things to make sure they would not get caught again."

After returning home on Halloween of 1969, Ed got a job working for the state of Pennsylvania as a custodian for a mental hospital in Luzerne County. The hospital got unionized and he became a steward, handling grievances.

After five years, he moved to Florida to organize for the American Federation of State, County, and Municipal Employees (AFSCME)—the largest public employees' trade union in the country—from Fort Lauderdale north to Jacksonville, Gainesville, and Tallahassee.

"I loved my job," Ed remembers. "It was different. I got to teach on weekends—about stewards' training, and organizing. I enjoyed meeting people. The University of Florida was my primary responsibility, which was huge. Florida did not want anyone unionized, like any other state government. It was eye-opening for me—entirely different than the military. The state was still mostly segregated back then. You went up to the panhandle, they'd call you 'Yankee,' and not in a nice way. I was exposed to many more black people than back in Pennsylvania. There were no blacks in my high school. It was an entirely different atmosphere for me in the service and in the unions."

Homesick, he returned to Luzerne County in the late seventies and went to work as a business agent handling contract negotiations for AFSCME. He also became a key labor operative in Pennsylvania political campaigns, running phone banks and canvassing operations. He worked congressional, gubernatorial, and presidential campaigns, including those for Bill Clinton, Michael Dukakis, John Kerry, and Barack Obama.

Once, in 1988, the Dukakis campaign arranged to plant him at a town hall event to lob a friendly question to the Massachusetts governor, Ed says, chuckling at the memory.

In 2012, he became president of the Wilkes–Barre Labor Council.

But despite his deep involvement in Democratic politics, Ed gradually found himself growing more and more disenchanted with the party. While he'd worked for Obama's election twice through the labor movement, Ed had not voted for him. He'd opted for Republican Ron Paul in 2008 and Gary Johnson, the Libertarian, in 2012.

In 2016, Ed's first choice was Jim Webb, the conservative former senator from Virginia who announced he would seek the Democratic nomination to run for president, but Webb dropped out early.

Ed thought Hillary Clinton and the Democrats were preoccupied with cultural issues he deemed trivial, like separate bathrooms for transsexuals. "To me there are more important issues than getting an extra door for transsexuals in public buildings. I worked with the gay and lesbian communities. But now, the trans stuff, it's every day in the paper. There's enough problems out there. Should this really be national news when there are no jobs and businesses are leaving? To me this issue is not important...I don't know where the Democrats are going. They're so far left. The party I grew up with certainly doesn't exist."

When the Wilkes–Barre Labor Council announced in April 2016, just before the Pennsylvania primary, that it was endorsing Hillary Clinton, Ed resigned as president and announced that he was voting for Donald Trump.

Though plenty of union rank and file in Pennsylvania were voting for Trump too, union leadership viewed Ed's move as a treasonous act. He had virtually outed himself by showing up at the raucous rally Trump held in April outside Wilkes-Barre that was attended by some twelve thousand people.

Reporters knew him and spotted him, and he agreed to do an interview with the popular local radio talk show host Sue Henry.

"People asked why I was there. I said, 'I'm here because I'm going to support Trump.' The next morning, I received a phone call from the union, asking if it was true I'd come out for Trump. I said it was, and to save them the embarrassment, I told them I'd resign."

But the union made him walk the plank. He was told he had to formally resign in front of his membership at the next meeting. "I think by that time almost everybody knew. We did the pledge, then I got up and said, 'As of today I'm officially resigning as president of the labor council, and the reason is, I've publicly endorsed Donald Trump for president. I did it on the radio. Live. I'm satisfied with my decision. Thank you and so long.'

"I'm one of the idiots who had enough guts to come out and support Trump."

Ed thinks Bill Clinton and Obama were complicit— ironically, along with the unions—in the decline of manufacturing in America and the loss of jobs to foreign countries.

"With Bill Clinton, it started with NAFTA and GATT. We lost probably twenty factories in Luzerne County because of NAFTA and GATT. I wondered why we were supporting these people, when all the jobs were leaving. Then Obama wanted to do the TPP. It all collapsed on me. I was fed up with both parties, so I looked at someone who wasn't a politician, and that was Trump. Trump started talking about trade. I know a lot of people who lost jobs after all the manufacturers left. There was a mass migration out of here. The jobs left because of the trade agreements. The jobs left! No one gave a shit. Politicians did not care.

"It was frustrating being in an office in a labor council and watching the jobs be wiped out, and no one cared, including the unions. It was all a swamp. And I made a living from being part of that system."

Ed concluded that the United States was too willing to accept an inevitable globalization of the economy.

"It meant my country was going to be dying. I had problems with how the European Union was created. Because no one had a vote. I'll be damned if the U.S. was going to be part of a UN globalized network, with the World Bank. I have problems with that. I actually believe that people direct the presidents what to do and say. What people? I don't know—industrial and banking heads. None of the EU citizens have any say. All the trade agreements we made—who was controlling our presidents that made the deals? Because they sure as hell weren't for the betterment of our country.

"The Republicans wanted cheap labor so they brought in the immigrants, which screwed the unions and other people. The Democrats brought all these people in to vote for them and keep their power, because a lot of the immigrants went to blue states to register to vote.

"At least I sleep better at night now. And Trump has been trying to change the trade agreements and bring jobs back. I have less respect for both political parties than I did a year ago. I knew Trump would take the heat he's taken."

Another factor that turned Ed toward Trump was the candidate's pledge to disengage from military quagmires abroad and put "America first."

"Especially as a veteran, I was fed up with all the wars going on," Ed says. "Whether it was Republicans or Democrats, in my mind they didn't care, as long as they got their political contributions. To be honest, I think all of us are fed up with all the wars that keep happening. We're tired. Since I've been born, we've been in a state of war almost all the time. When does it stop? We're pissing away all our money, building bombs that kill people, and we don't take care of veterans at home that need the help.

"I voted for Trump because he was a nonpolitician. Not because he was a liberal or conservative. Vietnam, Afghanistan, we're still involved in Iraq. If you want to fight something, bring it to an end one way or the other. The sad part is that whoever becomes president listens to the generals, and the generals, by nature, fight wars. And the biggest lobbyists are the defense contractors who spend a lot of money to keep wars going. We were warned by Eisenhower about the military-industrial complex. Nixon finally ended Vietnam because he was on his second term. War perpetuates itself. Is that how the rest of the vets feel? I don't know, but that's how I feel. All the money pissed away on wars could be used here to take care of the needs of people."

After he left the military, Ed swore he'd never own a gun, but he had a change of heart recently.

"I have problems with people taking shots at other people

all the time—whether it's at cops, the Vegas concert, that church in Texas. I never wanted to buy another gun after Vietnam. But the way things are going with the crazies in this country, I bought one last summer. Anything can happen, and I just want to have a weapon. Everybody around here has them."

Besides Trump's stance on trade and his America First agenda, several other issues that he pushed resonated with Ed. One was his flaying of the media. "People don't believe what they hear in the news anymore. For a whole bunch of reasons. I have to look at alternative sites like Drudge. I look at Breitbart. I don't get enough from what the major networks tell me. To me it's a propaganda machine. I read my two local papers cover to back, and occasionally *Time* or *Newsweek*. I'll listen to Hannity and Tucker on Fox, but I won't watch CNN or MSNBC. I listen to Alex Jones and Michael Savage."

Jones and Savage are syndicated radio talk show hosts noted for promoting conspiracy theories, which Ed readily entertains.

"I don't believe every theory that comes out until I do my own investigation," he explains. "Do I believe the official report on the JFK assassination? Absolutely not. And I read the Warren Commission, and fifteen or twenty books about the assassination.

"Do I believe 9/11 the way the government said? No, because I've watched documentaries about how the buildings were so tightly constructed. You'll never convince me that two planes caused the buildings to collapse."

Ed also questions the official versions of the Oklahoma City bombing and the Boston Marathon bombings, and embraces the unfounded theory that liberal billionaire George Soros paid Black Lives Matter $30 million to protest in Ferguson, Missouri, and Baltimore.

Voter fraud was another Trump issue that Ed approved of discussing. "Yes, there is a lot of voter fraud. I heard Obama say, 'All you immigrants come in and vote.' Governor Terry McAuliffe in Virginia let the prisoners vote. So yes, I believe Trump when he says there were 3.5 million illegal votes. I think that's somewhat conservative, actually. When I came home from Florida, there was an investigation of voter fraud in Luzerne County. Six or seven politicians were indicted for voter fraud. They'd fill out absentee ballots, hold them in abeyance, then release them as needed. So, is there voter fraud? Yeah. I assume it still goes on."

Ed is enjoying his retirement these days. He spends some of his time as chairman of the Luzerne County Arena Authority, which oversees the county's main indoor sports venue, Mohegan Sun Arena, outside Wilkes-Barre, where Trump packed the house at two rallies during the 2016 campaign.

In the summer, he likes going to county fairs, from Harrisburg east. He has lots of grass to cut at home. He's a big sports fan, especially any sport involving Penn State. He takes his four cats out for walks, and also helps tend to three cats at his girlfriend Rosalie's house.

Never married, Ed and Rosalie Zuba, seventy-one, have been together for forty-six years. He was twenty-four when they met. "When I worked my schedule, I was never home," he says. "It never came up that we should get married.

Rosalie gets $585 of Social Security a month now and she couldn't live without me. We opted not to have kids. We each took care of our parents until they died. She's the boss, like all women are. And I listen. I say, 'Yes, dear' and 'No, dear.' So we have very few arguments."

Like Ed, Rosalie voted for Trump, and it was the first time she ever voted in a presidential election. "She decided that on her own," Ed says. "I was shocked. She said she didn't like any of the others, or did not trust anyone else."

Marty Beccone

MARTY

Marty Beccone owns the 4th Street Pub, a popular bar and restaurant in Hazleton, Luzerne County's second city after Wilkes-Barre.

He has an American flag tattooed on his right shoulder and carries a .357 Magnum, mostly for protection after he closes 4th Street in the wee hours and makes his way to his car with the night's cash proceeds in hand.

He's a registered Independent who was disenchanted with President Obama and hungry for a change. "People weren't doing too well in our area under Obama," he says.

Though he'd voted for Bill Clinton in his first campaign for president, Marty was way tired of the Clintons by 2016 and never considered voting for Hillary.

"No, I feel she's a criminal," he says. "The whole email thing. There was classified information on the emails. If you had worked for the government and you had classified information on your server,' you'd be in jail. No decision. Somehow, she is not in trouble—at least for now."

On the other hand, Marty, who is fifty-four, had liked Donald Trump from the start, was taken by his pledge to cut taxes and get rid of Obamacare. "Renewing health insurance right now for me and my wife will cost fourteen hundred and fifty dollars for one month. That's insane! Eight years ago, I was paying seven hundred to seven hundred fifty a month. That was for my daughter too. Cutting corporate taxes will go in my pocket eventually. That's going to help everybody. Those were the main factors. If he lowers taxes, how could that be a bad thing?"

Hillary, Marty was convinced, wanted to raise his taxes. He thought Trump was more business-friendly and would be better on the economy. Marty didn't want a regular politician in the White House again, and Trump's business background appealed to him. He thought the country had fallen behind on Obama's watch. Trade deficits were too high, and he liked Trump's talk of negotiating better trade deals that put America's interests first. Cracking down on illegal immigration was important too. "When all that's settled, then we can think about helping others. I mean, people in this country need help too, don't they?"

As Trump's campaign developed, Marty came to see himself

as one of the forgotten people Trump said he stood for. "The middle class is the backbone of the country," Marty says. "The guy who runs the gas station, runs a store, or a restaurant. Like me! You're damn right, like me. That's who Trump is going to bat for."

Born and raised in New Jersey, Marty nonetheless had deep connections to Hazleton. His grandparents came over from Italy and settled in Hazleton, and his grandfather ran a popular Italian grocery there. "My grandfather had thirty guys in a butcher shop working for him in the twenties. He sold Italian meats and cheeses."

Marty came to Hazleton in 1982 to go to college at the city's Penn State campus. He lived in his aunt's apartment and met his future wife, Lisa. After graduating, he went to culinary arts school in Atlantic City, and then worked in a casino owned by none other than Donald Trump. He waited on Trump twice.

Marty stayed in Atlantic City until his daughter was born, whereupon the family moved back to Hazleton, and Marty opened an Italian grocery store, just as his grandfather had done. There was a bar next door that was not doing well; Marty thought he could spruce it up and turn it into a viable business. So he just closed the grocery store.

He made a go of it at the bar for a while, catering to a twenty-one- to twenty-five-year-old, largely single clientele. But when his customers aged, got married, and assumed responsibilities, he found that they came in less frequently, so after about ten years, Marty decided to broaden his customer base by buying another bar that also had a restaurant.

"That was 4th Street," he says. "It's a full-service restaurant. Everything's homemade. We make our own bread, smoked brisket, our own blue cheese dressing for the chicken wings. Only the pierogi [Polish ravioli] is not homemade, but I buy that from a guy who makes it himself, so it's like homemade. Our burgers are made from fresh ground beef. I did a roast pork the other night. Roasted it for eight hours. I mean, it just falls apart. We also make our own breaded mac and cheese."

The bar is crowded and smoky, and there is leakage into the token nonsmoking dining room. Pool leagues on Thursday through Saturday nights make the joint jump. Sunday through Wednesday is not as busy, but Marty has a loyal, regular crowd, and business is still solid, bolstered by a steady flow of take-out orders.

He offers his daily specials on Facebook, along with a steady flow of pro-Trump political posts.

Marty's wife, Lisa, helps out at 4th Street. "She's the director of ambience," he says, laughing. "She comes in, looks around, and says 'You'd better clean that' if she notices some dirt or dust somewhere. She tries the food and critiques it. She does the decor. I'm the bartender and the head chef, basically. I don't cook on a regular basis, but I make the specialties I like."

Marty and Lisa have been married for over thirty years. "You want to know our secret?" he asks. "Make sure your wife is your best friend. If not, it ain't ever gonna last."

Though all four of his grandparents came to the United States from Italy, Marty does not consider himself an Italian American. "People ask, 'What nationality are you?' I'm an

American! That's a thing with me—I believe that people from this country need to say, 'I'm an American.' That's what'll make this country great again. That's called national pride."

It was that national pride, Marty says, that moved him to get the flag tattooed on his shoulder in 2014.

He was raised Catholic, but is basically laissez-faire on religion. "I firmly believe there's a higher power. I totally believe there is a God. I don't know if Christianity is the right religion. It could be Buddhism, or whatever. There's religion everywhere. Every culture has it, so that makes me think there is a higher power. But it doesn't mean their God's right and mine's wrong. I was brought up Catholic, so I believe in Catholicism, but I actually believe in all religions."

On Marty's issues list, cutting taxes and getting rid of Obamacare were more important than curbing illegal immigration, but he was still concerned about it and favored Trump's wall at the Mexican border.

"I think the physical barrier would help," Marty says. "We need to protect ourselves. Any device to protect ourselves from illegal immigration, we should do. We can't have open borders. A system needs to be in place. Democrats want open borders because the more immigrants that come in, they vote Democrat for the most part. So you increase your base."

Family migration has to be curbed, he adds. "Someone comes here legally. He's able to bring his mother and father, his brother and all his family and also his children. Those people, in turn, are allowed to bring their family. And it never ends. So, in effect, there's an open border. At what point do we draw the line? That's my point. My thought would be, my wife and my daughter, and that's it."

Marty approves of Trump's attempt to restrict immigration from certain Muslim countries. "It wasn't a Muslim ban, as the media called it. It was extreme vetting of people coming here from certain countries. I think it was justified. Extreme vetting is basically trying to keep people likely to do something bad to hurt us out of our country. I agree with it. Sadly, there's a large group of people in the world who don't like Americans, for whatever the reason might be."

Basically, he thinks the existing laws against illegal immigration haven't been enforced aggressively enough.

Marty cites the 2006 murder of a Hazleton man, which provoked the city's famed crackdown on illegal immigration and triggered the rise of Congressman Lou Barletta, before the rise of Trump. "That, in a nutshell, is why illegal immigration is wrong. If you enforce it, maybe you save one life. Isn't that worth it? That happened in Hazleton, which is just one pimple on Pennsylvania's butt."

But Marty says the Hispanics who have poured into Hazleton over the past fifteen years and made it a majority-minority city have had a positive influence on the community.

"I see them as being like the immigrants from the twenties. My grandfather came over from Italy and opened an Italian grocery store. My great-uncle had a barbershop. I'm all for that. The Hispanics here today are trying to come and live the American dream. Ninety percent are here legally, and contribute to the economy. I have a guy who comes into my place and he doesn't speak a word of English. A Dominican guy. He comes in and hugs me. Spends his money. That's as good as it gets. Other people get sour and say, 'Look at the crime!' But crime is everywhere. Every city has a bad section. So, you don't go to that section! That's the way it is."

If many whites have fled Hazleton feeling threatened by the new Hispanic arrivals, Marty does not. "I don't feel threatened," he says.

He thought the 2016 election underscored the rural–urban divide in America and differing views on government dependence.

"There's a different set of values. Generally, the people in the cities are Democratic voters. Why is that? It's the percentage of people who get government assistance. For example, look at what portion of New York City gets some type of government assistance, and then look at what portion of rural America gets government assistance. I think it all comes down to dollars and cents. If you're on welfare, why would you vote for someone who could limit the amount of government assistance you get? That would be biting the hand that feeds you. That's where I think the divide is. Pennsylvania goes ninety percent Republican except for Philadelphia and Pittsburgh, which go Democrat, and that's how Pennsylvania has been a Democratic state for the most part."

Marty defended Trump's coarse language and vulgar comments directed at various women over the years, but thought those controversies, along with the #MeToo movement, had stimulated a healthy dialogue about sexual harassment.

Invoking the locker-room defense, he dismissed the *Access Hollywood* tape of 2005 that rocked Trump's campaign when it leaked in 2016.

"Come on, you're a guy, you've been in a locker room.

Guys talk!" he says. "A pretty girl goes by, guys talk! And you know what? Girls talk too. I see it in my bar.

"The sexual harassment thing, if you're using that as power—as in, 'You'll never work in this town again'—that's criminal. If someone was messing with me, I would say, 'Quit doing that.' Going forward in our country, I think if someone touches someone inappropriately, they're going to be called out immediately. Women now feel empowered to do something about it, and if anything, that's a huge positive for our culture."

As for Trump's use of profanity, his combative style, and his habit of insulting his rivals and enemies, Marty thinks this merely reflects today's society as it is. "Isn't that what America is now? Everything is crude, lewd, and all on social media. I think people related to that in the campaign. I don't know anybody that doesn't curse, do you?"

One issue Marty says he differs with Trump on is gay rights. "Whose business is it to tell someone who they can marry? No one's business. You're damn right it isn't. I disagree with Trump on that."

And there's one other thing: "The only other negative I have is that I'd mark him down on the tweeting. He should dial that back a little bit."

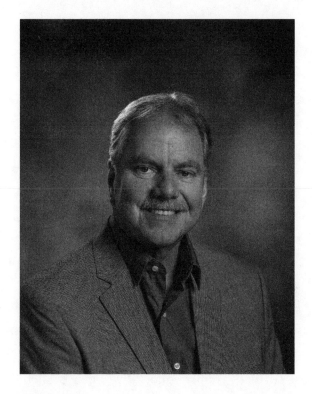

Brian Langan

BRIAN

Brian Langan, fifty-seven, recently retired after working as a detective with the Pennsylvania State Police for more than twenty-five years.

He's beaten stage four cancer and drives a 2001 red Corvette. Life is fragile, and Brian means to make the most of it.

The youngest son of a father who was operations director of the AFL-CIO in Washington, DC, Brian was raised to be a Democrat, but he grew dissatisfied with the party and became a Republican in order to vote for Ronald Reagan in 1980.

"I felt I didn't leave the Democratic Party—the Democratic Party left me," Brian says. "I think that's what happened in Luzerne County: more and more people realized the Democrats weren't helping them. And the establishment Republicans didn't seem to be fighting for me at all either. I thought, *Washington is broke, and I need someone to go down there with a sledgehammer.* That was Donald Trump."

Trump won Brian over with his answer when, at a 2015 debate with the other Republican presidential candidates, Megyn Kelly asked him about disparaging remarks he'd made in the past about women, such as calling them "fat pigs" and "dogs."

"Only Rosie O'Donnell," Trump quipped before suggesting to Kelly that she lighten up and not be so politically correct. "I think the big problem this country has is being politically correct," Trump said. "I've been challenged by so many people and I don't frankly have the time for total political correctness, and to be honest with you, this country doesn't have time either."

When Brian heard that answer, he stood up and cheered. "Megyn Kelly went after his personal character and Trump didn't back down. He didn't answer the question like a politician. He answered it like a man. He was standing up for himself."

And he loved Trump's broadside on political correctness, finding it "*so* refreshing. Political correctness will kill us all. They say if you see something, say something. But if you did, you'd be sued by the Justice Department because that guy just happened to be of Middle Eastern descent."

Brian felt politically and culturally distant from President

Obama, but got no comfort from the Republican establishment either. "We weren't getting anywhere with Romney, McCain, or Paul Ryan. More and more, I open my paycheck and there's less and less of mine. I feel they're just giving my money away."

As examples of giveaways, Brian liked to cite familiar conservative tropes like the "Obama free phone thing" for welfare recipients, or the Solyndra fiasco. The Federal Communications Commission established discounted phone service for low-income people decades ago, and the program was expanded under George W. Bush in 2008 to include cell phones, and expanded further under Obama. Solyndra, a startup solar panel company, was the first recipient of a loan guarantee under Obama's economic stimulus program. The company received $535 million but later filed for bankruptcy.

"I'm not against welfare," Brian says. "I'm a caring person. But my daughters and grandkids have to pay for all this."

For Brian, Solyndra symbolized an effete brand of environmentalism that seemed to prioritize a do-gooder, save-the-planet ethos over the practical need for good jobs at good wages. He bemoans the loss of solid manufacturing jobs in the United States, like the dress factories that used to exist in northeast Pennsylvania when he was growing up.

What could Trump do about that? Perhaps nothing, but his talk of America taking it in the shorts on trade deals and being strangled by excessive regulations rang true for Brian.

"The EPA is out of control and it's costing me money. I'm getting ready to retire and I have toys I want to buy. Like, when they do environmental impact studies on bridges: they're more concerned [with] what happens to the frog under the bridge than they are about building the damn bridge."

Brian says he and his neighbors are willing to work, but there just aren't enough jobs, and one reason is that too many undocumented immigrants are coming in to take them.

"People who say we have free, open borders because that's who we are? No, we're not morons who say it doesn't matter, and that anyone can work here. It's not an excuse to make bad decisions."

The youngest of three boys, Brian grew up in Wyoming, Pennsylvania, a township about five miles north of Wilkes-Barre. His father, James Langan, was a letter carrier by day, a railroad engineer by night, and a union activist at both positions. James's brother-in-law, a coal miner, had been killed in an accident on the job. James viewed his main job as being a mailman, and it was not long before his union, the National Association of Letter Carriers, sent him to its national headquarters in Washington, DC, and put him on its executive board. Later, the NALC named him as its representative to the AFL-CIO, for which he served as operations director.

A pro-life Democrat, the elder Langan was steeped in party politics and forged friendships with a variety of Democratic notables, including his local congressman, the exuberant Dan Flood—known on Capitol Hill as "Dapper Dan" due to his trademark waxed mustache—and Senator Daniel Patrick Moynihan of New York. Brian treasures a photo of his father in the Oval Office with President John F. Kennedy, and he remembers Flood arranging a tour of the Nixon White House for him and his father.

"I was a little impressed and a little scared because my father knew his way around the White House," Brian recalls. "I was twelve. Dad told me he did not like Nixon because he had ice water in his veins. Dad was union as can be. I always thought I was a Democrat too. My father used to say to me, 'Help those who need help.'"

Jim Langan retired in 1963 and moved back to Pennsylvania, when Brian was only two. He immersed himself in Wyoming township affairs, getting elected to the local school board and making an unsuccessful run for mayor. He died in 1979 at age seventy-four, when Brian was in the eleventh grade. Brian's mother, Frances Langan, a housewife, died a short time later.

"My strongest memories growing up are just of living in a bucolic small town. I'd go out and play, walk a few blocks to the park, ride my bike everywhere. People would bring their kids to learn to drive in Wyoming because the streets were wide. Every neighbor knew you, and if you did something wrong, they would tell your parents."

Hurricane Agnes hit on June 23, 1972, and that was unforgettable. The Susquehanna River raged over its banks and deluged Wilkes-Barre and surrounding areas, causing over $1 billion in damage, and several deaths. Dan Flood led the relief efforts, using his seniority in the House to full advantage and bringing in President Nixon to survey the damage. "It took a Flood to tame a flood," the congressman liked to say afterward.

After graduating from high school, Brian briefly attended Luzerne County Community College, but that didn't go well, so he enrolled in a travel industry training school in Pittsburgh. He was hired by Air Florida to work as a reservation agent and was sent to Miami.

Brian lived across from the Doral Country Club and partied heavily. One of his favorite bars was called Gator Kicks Longneck Saloon, which proudly displayed a poster of a teenage Donna Rice, posing with a Confederate flag draped over one of her breasts, the other exposed. This was about ten years before she became nationally known for her entanglement with Democratic presidential candidate Gary Hart in a scandal that forced Hart, a former senator from Colorado, to drop out of the race. "Miami was culture shock," Brian says. "I was living the high life. I would watch as they closed down streets to film *Miami Vice*."

In 1982, one of Air Florida's planes crashed into the 14th Street Bridge in Washington, DC, and plunged into the Potomac River, killing seventy-four people. The airline went out of business shortly thereafter, and Brian was out of a job.

He returned home to Luzerne County and drove a water delivery truck for a time before catching on with the state police in 1992. Making a water delivery to a school one day, Brian met his future wife, Lorena, a teacher who would sign for the water. They have been married twenty-nine years and have a daughter, Meghan, who works as a state prison guard in Luzerne.

In addition to his red Corvette, Brian has already started to acquire some of those toys he's been coveting for his retirement, such as a Harley motorcycle and a camper he can tour the country with. He'll take the camper to state parks, ride the Harley during summers at home, and sometimes trailer it to biker destinations like Daytona Beach, Florida.

As a hobby, Brian likes to make his own bullets for the 40-millimeter gun he carries, a practice called reloading. After you fire a shot, you take the primer out of the old shell casing, put new gunpowder in its place, and then put a new bullet over it.

Brian isn't in full retirement mode yet, but he's easing into it, having taken a job as a compliance officer for an amusement gaming business after resigning from the state police in early 2018. The new job isn't as stressful as his police work, when he was a detective working mostly undercover as a liquor enforcement agent, developing vice cases in bars to combat illegal gambling and underage drinking.

He says his twenty-five years in law enforcement have made him more conservative. "It made me see things more black-and-white, and less gray."

Brian decided it was Donald Trump who had the best chance of bringing back good jobs to the country, and of protecting other rights he cared about, like the right to carry a gun.

"You are in NRA country here. People have been hunting with their grandfathers and great-grandfathers for generations. I think those traditions would have been threatened if the other side had won. They wanted an Australian-type gun ban. They could have done a lot of damage with executive orders and a new Supreme Court. They were chipping away. The 'disarm America' people are not done. I'm very fortunate that under a federal law passed after 9/11, as a bona fide member of law enforcement, I can carry a concealed weapon in any state I want. So, I do carry a concealed weapon all the time. But you shouldn't have to be a police officer to have that special right. I don't agree with that."

Brian tells of a gruesome crime that happened at his neighborhood grocery store in 2017, when a sixteen-year-old boy went berserk and stabbed a woman who was in the store at the time. "You can't tell me she doesn't have a basic right to defend herself," he says.

Trump seemed a good cultural fit for Brian too. He liked the candidate's "Make America Great Again" slogan for the nostalgia it evoked of better, simpler times.

"When I went to school, I believed America was founded for good, always wanted to do good; we helped others and went to war for other countries. In the past administration, it became more and more, 'There is something about America that is not great.' But it really is. We are a great country, great workers, great history, and very generous. But Obama went on an apology tour. For what? All we ever did was try to help people.

"People started thinking about how to get on disability and who's going to pay for my kid. They tell you it's bad to say 'Mom, dad, apple pie, and baseball.' You find people who'd be going to the great universities and saying this was a classic example of colonialism and stealing people's rights.

"I believe it was a slow pot to boil. People got sick of some academic telling them if they would just shut up and listen, the social utopia would materialize. It was 'They know better than we do.' They said we're hurting the planet by wanting someone to get a job rather than promoting animal rights.

"Wasn't it better when everyone went to work and had a

job and was happy and people had a little money in their pocket? Now the elites are telling me that was the worst life that there could be."

Brian, like many Trump supporters, thought the media was biased against the candidate in its coverage of the campaign. Then Brian added an interesting twist: that journalists, in their zeal to sink Trump's candidacy, reported on what he said too literally rather than trying to glean, as Brian says he and other supporters did, what Trump actually *meant* to say. So, while his rhetoric may have sounded incendiary or racist to some people, it really was not, if you knew how to decode it.

"Trump's rhetoric was over the top sometimes, it's true, but that never concerned me at all," Brian says. "I never doubted him. A lot of it was just his New York style. If he said 'Build a wall,' as long as I have a secure border, I knew it may not be all wall. When he talked about Mexico sending killers and rapists, I knew he did not mean all of them. I think the media exaggerated that. And what he said on the *Access Hollywood* tape about coming on to women, that didn't bother me either. On the set of a movie, things are said. I'm sure Jane Fonda has said worse. I think it's hypocritical. They tried every gotcha in the book against Trump, but he was Teflon."

Brian says Trump supporters totally lost trust in the mainstream media's ability to tell it straight. He took his daughter to Trump's second rally in Luzerne County, shortly before the election. "In the center was the press. I'm pointing out John King from CNN to my daughter. The crowd was chanting 'CNN sucks' even before Trump prompted them. I don't know what happened to the media. They used to report facts; now they have an agenda. I didn't fall for that, and I don't think many people in northeastern Pennsylvania did either."

Brian gets his news from Drudge, Breitbart, Fox, and occasionally MSNBC, to keep an eye on what the Left is up to. As examples of bias, Brian cites Donna Brazile, then a CNN analyst and interim Democratic National Committee chair, leaking a presidential debate question to the Hillary Clinton campaign and a reporter for Politico sending an article to Clinton campaign chair John Podesta before publishing it. The reporter, Glenn Thrush, said he was fact-checking the story, not giving Podesta approval of it.

A study by Harvard Kennedy School's Shorenstein Center on Media, Politics, and Public Policy found that media coverage of Trump during the general election campaign—from the second week of August 2016 to the day before Election Day—was more negative than Clinton's coverage. The Trump coverage was judged 77 percent negative to 23 percent positive. But over the course of the entire two-year campaign, it was Clinton who received the most negative coverage. The study found that overall, 62 percent of her press was considered negative and 38 percent positive, while Trump's was 56 percent negative to 44 percent positive.

TRUMP WOMEN

Lynette Villano with her candidate

LYNETTE

Lynette Villano, a seventy-two-year-old widow and clerk for the Wyoming Valley Sanitary Authority, in Wilkes-Barre, is so enamored with Donald Trump that during the 2016 campaign, her coworkers called her "Mrs. Trump."

"I came out for Trump the day he came down that escalator in Trump Tower," she recalls. "I went right online and got some pins. I did it to see what kind of reaction I'd get when I wore them in public. Most of the time it was positive. Sometimes it was relief—like, 'Oh my God, here's another Trump supporter I can talk to.' People liked Trump because he had the answers to all our frustrations!"

Lynette was not feeling good about the country under President Obama. The economy was doing poorly, at least in Luzerne County. She thought he was apologizing for America too much, and she was disgusted with Obamacare.

She is quick to clarify that her opposition to Obama had nothing to do with his being black, and she didn't like it when people inferred that. She liked him as a person. She just didn't like his policies, or the way he governed.

Lynette thought electing Hillary Clinton would have meant an effective Obama third term. And besides, she says, "It was so insulting to women that we were made to feel we had to vote for Hillary just because she's a woman."

There was also, she thought, a cultural discord that had developed in the Obama years. There was too much illegal immigration around and about, too much political correctness, and not enough respect for traditional values.

"In my era, you respected authority," Lynette says. "Today, a lot of the standards we grew up with are gone—the church, the flag. And these police shootings. I'm extremely sensitive about that. I'm trying to understand this Black Lives Matter movement. But I'm not black, and I grew up in a Catholic girls' school, so maybe I can't."

The Obama presidency reminded Lynette of the Jimmy Carter "malaise" years in the late 1970s, another time when people weren't feeling good about the country, before the sunny arrival of Ronald Reagan. In fact, she felt that Trump was Reaganesque. After all, Reagan was an actor who wasn't taken seriously, just as Trump wasn't. Both offered hope, she thought.

★　　★　　★

Lynette was born and raised in Wilkes-Barre, the eldest of three children. Her father left the family when she was about four years old, forcing her mother, who worked in a shoe factory, to pack up the kids and move in with her parents. Lynette's grandfather was a Wilkes-Barre police detective, while her grandmother essentially raised her, along with her younger sister and brother.

Lynette grew up in a mostly German Wilkes-Barre neighborhood that she describes as "like *Happy Days,*" the 1970s television program that depicted an idealized version of Middle America in the 1950s and '60s. With the help of some adults, she and her friends started a neighborhood newspaper that they sold for two cents a copy.

She went to a Catholic school for twelve years, and the church was dominant in her life. It was mass every Sunday, holy days, confession every week, stations of the cross, first Friday mass, novenas, May crowning, processions on Holy Thursday.

"Anything Catholic, I was there," Lynette remembers. "When we were in eighth grade, it was a big deal that we would be allowed to help clean the altar and lay out the vestments for the priest for Sunday. After all, women were not allowed to even touch the chalice, so this was very meaningful and special…Until I met my husband, I don't think I knew anyone who wasn't Catholic."

In 1965, Lynette married Ronald Villano, an auto mechanic. They were married for more than fifty years and had two children: a daughter, who now works as a career counselor at Wilkes University in Wilkes-Barre, and a son, who is a chef. Lynette's husband died of a cerebral hemorrhage in August 2016, three months before the election.

Lynette has been involved in local politics for thirty years, starting out as a volunteer for Arlen Specter, the late Pennsylvania senator who was elected as a Republican but later became a Democrat. She's been on the Luzerne County Republican Committee for over twenty-five years, and was the first woman to become county chair. She was also a longtime member of the Republican State Committee. Lynette parlayed her political connections into a job on the sanitary authority, which runs the wastewater treatment plant for Luzerne County. She is a dyed-in-the-wool Republican, and while she'd voted for many establishment types in the past, Trump's roguishness appealed to her.

The county is only a few hours' drive from New York, and Lynette would visit the city regularly over the years. She knew all about Trump and liked him. She had long admired his business success and thought he could apply that to boost the economy. She wanted an outsider, a nonpolitician. And she was drawn to his signature campaign issue of curbing illegal immigration because it had special resonance in Luzerne, where Lou Barletta had gotten the topic national attention ten years earlier as mayor of Hazleton. Lynette was a big fan of Lou's.

She liked Trump's moxie, his feistiness. "He wasn't afraid to say anything. The political correctness has gotten so bad that people were so intimidated. People felt like they were getting things shoved down their throat. They thought Trump was talking common sense, and that maybe he'd bring jobs back."

Lynette decided to jump in with both feet and run to be elected a Trump delegate to the Republican National Convention in Cleveland. She ran successfully on a slate with two other women, which they called Women for Trump. They felt that name was significant because their candidate had been deluged with criticism during the campaign for having called women "dogs" and "fat pigs" in the past. Lynette thought that was much ado about nothing and that it was important to show that Trump had plenty of supporters who were women.

"The three of us running for delegate would stand out at the mall in Wilkes-Barre with our signs and we'd spend the afternoon there, people beeping their horns as they passed by," Lynette remembers. "You couldn't believe the energy! Sometimes Hillary supporters would drive by and give us the finger."

As she talked politics daily with people she met, Lynette kept having to douse other Trump brush fires, such as when the *Access Hollywood* tape came out a month before the election. Lynette gave Trump a pass on that: "I did not approve of what he said on the tape. But something he said thirty years ago did not really bother me. They used it to make him look bad. Men in locker rooms do say things. Women too!" Lynette was prone to exaggerating the age of the tape to lessen its significance. When the tape was revealed in 2016, it was eleven years old, not thirty.

She took the same line when a string of women came forward during the campaign to claim that Trump had sexually abused them years ago. Why hadn't they come forward at the time the incidents supposedly happened? Lynette asked. And she complained that the Trump accusers were given credibility by the media, while the women who had accused Bill Clinton of similar offenses were largely dismissed as white trash.

Along with other women of a certain age, Lynette would come to think that the emerging #MeToo movement was going too far. "I had things done to me when I was a young woman, but it was dealt with at the time, not years later. When you come out years later and ruin a guy's reputation, I have trouble with that."

Lynette also found herself playing defense following a steady stream of Trump's shocking statements, such as when he questioned the legitimacy of Barack Obama's birth certificate and said that John McCain was not a war hero and that Mexicans coming to the United States were rapists— statements so outrageous they would have destroyed any other candidate, but which came to be regarded as par for the Trump course.

"Yes, he said these things," Lynette conceded, but, pointing to the announcement speech, she added, "He did not say *all* Mexicans. Some things were picked out and used over and over again. We say *some* Mexicans. It's the word 'illegal.' We don't want the illegals to come. All our ancestors came here legally, and people think that's not what's happening today. Then you look at these refugees. It's a complicated world."

Lynette learned to spin like an amateur Kellyanne Conway when talking to Trump detractors or to journalists who would come to town and interview her as a gung ho Trump supporter. Just as Brian Langan believed, Lynette would say you had to learn how to decode Trump, to know what he meant and what he didn't. She thought Trump's insults were mostly amusing, and didn't take them literally, or seriously. It bothered her when the media would blow up Trump's provocative statements when she and his other supporters *knew* he didn't really mean what he said. They just thought he was a different candidate who was speaking his mind in a refreshing way.

"Unlike Hillary, Trump didn't talk down to people, and we liked that," Lynette says. "And the Russians didn't make us vote for him!"

Still, sometimes it was hard to be a Trump supporter.

"When people put Trump down all the time, it was hard not to think they were putting *you* down too," Lynette says. "We were constantly being made to feel uneducated if we supported Trump. We felt like elitists were laughing at us. That hurt me."

And there were personal costs as well. "It wasn't easy to be with Trump. I went against people in my own party, I lost friends, and it caused a break within my family."

The family rift was especially painful to Lynette. It involved a clash over Trump that Lynette had with her grandson, Connor Mulvey, now a student at Tulane University Law School.

As the 2016 general election campaign unfolded, Connor was starting his senior year as an undergraduate at Tulane.

The day after the election, Lynette texted her grandson, saying how happy she was that Trump had won. Connor replied in a manner that she didn't think was respectful or appropriate when addressing his grandmother.

"I guess you can probably figure out that I'm very happy today," Lynette began. "Donald Trump is to your generation what Ronald Reagan was to ours. I am so fortunate to have been part of both...He defied conventional wisdom at every turn...Hopefully I will be going to the inauguration."

Connor did not hold back with his reply.

"Donald Trump is a bigoted imbecile who tapped into the racism and ignorance in America," he texted. "You're right, he is like Ronald Reagan. He's going to leave this country in ruins and completely ignore minorities' problems. The fact that he 'won' this election is a blemish on the history of the United States. I will not be recognizing him as my president, because much like George W. Bush, he failed to win the popular vote. The only difference is that I believe Bush was a good person who was manipulated by those around him. Donald is an arrogant asshole with a history of abuse, mistreatment, and greed. He and his supporters should be ashamed of themselves, but it's evident they lack the self-reflective capabilities to do so. I want you to think long and hard about what you've aided in. My LGBT friends are scared. My Muslim friends are scared. My Hispanic friends are scared. My female friends are scared. I'm scared. The fact that you've gone along with his disgraceful rhetoric the entire way through disappoints me to no end. Congratulations, you've damaged America. I hope it was worth it."

But Lynette did not back down. "I've saved America and I am very proud," she wrote in reply. "It is your future that kept me strong and made me work even harder. BTW, I also have LGBT and women friends and legal Hispanics that support Donald Trump. Eighty percent of the country feels we are headed in the wrong direction and that is the poll that mattered. Us uneducated deplorables are a lot smarter than you think. We are tired of the corruption and we aren't going to take it anymore. Just look at the protesters in the streets—that is why Donald Trump won. Every four to eight years, we have an orderly transfer of power. It is what makes our country great. So calm down and be proud you live in the greatest country in the world. Learn how to be grateful for all the opportunity you have and especially a family that cares about you. All I know is my mother would be very happy and proud of me."

To which Connor replied, "You didn't save America, you damned it. Trump goes against core American values and you bought into his race-baiting. You can keep lying to yourself and think that people want Trump, but he lost the popular vote... You don't have to deal with the repercussions of his presidency. I do. My entire generation does. You're completely brainwashed and incapable of seeing a rational truth... The U.S. is not the greatest country in the world anymore. Last night confirmed that. We aren't going to be for a long time. Get a grip on reality. If you deplorables are as smart as you think you are, maybe you would realize how dangerous Republican economic plans are. Now I'll be entering the job market under one. Thanks for that. But that's nothing compared to what my marginalized friends will have to go through. Thanks to you and your kind, hatred and bigotry have been normalized and legitimized. I hope you're proud of that."

Lynette responded, "Till the day I die I will stand by my decision to work for and help elect Donald Trump. You can describe it in any twisted way you want, but I know I did the right thing. You may have a college education, but you need life experience with it to really learn about life. I have very good friends and we totally disagreed on this election, but we respected each other's opinion. You know better than anyone the popular vote doesn't matter at all. It's the electoral college, and when finished he will have over three hundred votes. Massive government failure and the average working person feeling left out is why he won. It's a shame that fancy college doesn't teach you common courtesy and tolerance for others' opinions. I still love you and am proud of you, even though I do not agree with any of your views."

But Connor had the last word. "This college has taught me more than you'll ever know about politics. I respected you voting for McCain and Romney, but absolutely not Trump. I am truly ashamed. You're too far gone at this point, and I haven't seen an original thought come from you in years regarding politics. I guarantee you would be in an uproar if Hillary won the electoral but lost the popular. The government hasn't failed, Republicans have. Your party has become the party of the KKK and neo-Nazis, and if you're too blind to see that I feel sorry for you. Maybe if you went to college you would realize that Trump is the worst candidate in modern history, and that he's up there with George Wallace and David Duke. Maybe you would also realize your party wants to totally infringe on basic civil rights of women, the LGBT community, and minorities. If you had more interaction with them you might be able to sympathize."

The fallout from this exchange still reverberates with Lynette. Despite the harsh texts, she sent her grandson Christmas presents in 2016; he returned them. She was not invited to attend his graduation from Tulane in May 2017, or his twenty-first-birthday celebration the following day. Still, when Connor took out a $10,000 loan after graduating and needed a cosigner, Lynette obliged him.

There were other political divides in her family. Her sister, a Democrat, unfriended Lynette on Facebook over her pro-Trump posts, though they remain in touch in other ways. And when her uncle in Michigan died recently and she drove out for the funeral, Lynette discovered another split there. She stayed with a cousin who had a sign in her yard that read "We support refugees and our Muslim neighbors." But, because she was wearing her Trump pin, others in the family came up to tell her that they too had voted for the president.

"I'm sure I'm not the only one who has had to deal with estrangement from family members because of the election," Lynette says. "Does it hurt? More than I can put into words... This is the reality of how divided we are in this country—friendships lost, and in my case the relationship I had with my grandson. Politics has been part of my life for years, but this is the first time I have had to deal with this reaction. People so dislike our president there is no tolerance for anyone who supports him. Sadly, this is the world we live in today."

Donna Kowalczyk

DONNA

Donna Kowalczyk, sixty, has run a hair salon in the Wilkes-Barre area for more than forty years. She is married with three grown children, and lives upstairs from her salon on a decaying city block that she struggles to defend against incursions from drug dealers, car thieves, and prostitutes.

She was a lifelong Democrat who switched parties to vote for Donald Trump in the Republican primary of 2016. Donna is hoping the president can give a jolt to the local economy, which lags far behind the rest of the country. "Our area never recovered from the 2008 recession," she says. "Our

130

homes are worth nothing. I live on a block with four empty lots and four boarded-up houses. We need to do something. We need jobs here."

Going back to college late in life, Donna wrote a paper on Trump. "I was very impressed [with] how he gave jobs to women. He's kind. I heard about things he's done for people. I heard him speak on Jay Leno years ago about what he said he would do if he ran for president. He said, 'We'll take care of ourselves before we take care of others.' We're still spending like we're the richest country in the world, and we're not."

Donna was born and raised in Luzerne County, and her father worked as a subcontractor for the local gas company. He was disabled in the 1950s and became an alcoholic. Her mother worked for a cigar factory and then a sewing factory. Donna has a daughter, twenty-four, who's pursuing a career as an athletic trainer. One of her twin boys, who are twenty-five, works as a software developer in Wisconsin; the other manages an AutoZone franchise in Wilkes-Barre.

Donna went to beauty school and opened her first salon when she was just nineteen, in Kingston, a borough outside Wilkes-Barre, in 1977. Her husband, Jim, worked as head of maintenance at Wilkes University. That enabled her to later take courses there at a discount, and she gradually accumulated seventy-six credits. She concentrated on business courses and wrote her paper on Trump. "He appealed to me because he was promoting women," Donna says.

She's been a big believer in holistic practices for thirty years and talks excitedly about a recent workshop she attended. "There were New Age people there, tree huggers, herbalists, and psychics. We did a ritual for the earth. You sit in a circle and pray. Forty years ago, ninety-nine percent of people at these things would have been hippies, and I bet I'm the only Republican in that group." She is incorporating crystal healing into her hairdressing practice, working to develop a "soul-enhancing haircut," for which she would take crystals to a customer's scalp to "help balance their aura... You see? I'm totally opposite of what a Trump supporter should be!"

Donna spends much of her time trying to clean up her own street in downtown Wilkes-Barre and, by extension, the city itself.

"We have two universities and a community college and a branch of Penn State in Wilkes-Barre, but we have nothing else—no companies, no one willing to pay a decent salary that someone could pay off a student loan with," she says. "There are literally no jobs here. Our unemployment rate is probably four times higher than it really is. People just quit looking. We used to have the coal industry and a lot of factories. We don't have that anymore. If you get a job around here for eleven dollars an hour, you're doing fantastic. But how can you live on eleven dollars an hour? You see veterans here with canes waiting to get into the VA. It's horrible. I think Trump has the business sense that if anybody can fix it, he can."

Donna has lived in her house at 419 South River Street since 1994. There are "God Bless America" and "Let Freedom Ring" signs hanging on her front porch. The house is assessed for $121,500, but she says the actual market value is only $50,000. Taxes are high and she has to pay $2,000 a year in flood insurance, because she lives a few blocks from the Susquehanna River.

When she first bought the house, the hookers on the street wore high heels and fishnets, but now they're usually just in jeans, Donna says wryly when discussing how her neighborhood has evolved over the years.

Conducting a tour of her block, she points to a mostly empty lot adjacent to her house that has a pizza joint; it closed after the recession but reopened in 2015. A Lutheran church across the street has just a dozen or so regular members, half of whom use walkers, Donna says. There's a tire business directly behind her house, which sometimes stacks its tires along her back fence, causing a smell.

"When I complained to the owner, he told me if I was stupid enough to live here, I deserved everything I get." Across from the tire dealer is a variety store nicknamed "Grab and Stab." The locals say that means you might get stabbed by the owner if you try and steal something.

Many of the houses on Donna's block are boarded up, unoccupied, or have squatters living in them. One attractive brick house had a fire in it several years ago. It sold for $38,500, and a buyer made initial repairs, but then walked away and never moved in. A six-unit building has been for sale for ten years. One big house recently sold for $19,000.

Demographically, the block is about half white, half minority. "In another year or so, it'll be eighty-twenty minority," Donna says.

As a leader of her neighborhood association, Donna has been working for years to try and make improvements to her block. She and a neighbor, Lisa McGahee, have had press conferences to call attention to blight, crime, and prostitution on the street. But getting help from the authorities has been difficult. A police commander once dismissed Donna and Lisa as "hysterical housewives."

The association was an outgrowth of an attempt to get Wilkes-Barre into the federal Weed and Seed program, a crime-fighting initiative administered by the Department of Justice. But the effort failed when Wilkes-Barre did not hire a required number of police officers, thereby losing grants that would have been worth at least $600,000.

Donna says that in 1995, a bullet crashed through her daughter's window, and a woman was killed on the corner. The woman had gone to buy drugs, and two competing gangs had a shoot-out. In 2001, Donna's car was stolen from her driveway and later set on fire. "We took it as a threat to quit Weed and Seed," she says, crying as she tells the story.

To chronicle her time in Wilkes-Barre, Donna is writing a novel called *Wild Berry*. "I don't know who the good guys are and who the bad guys are anymore."

Despite the crime in her neighborhood, Donna doesn't own a gun and says she never will. "I think people should be able to protect their homes and their family, but it gives me an uncomfortable feeling when you go to the drugstore and see people with guns in their holster. It's like the Wild West around here now.

"I used to be the most liberal person you could imagine, fighting for everyone else's rights—before I moved here. Then you're exposed to unsavory people, and working your ass off to get by. These people come in from out of town, living off Section 8, and getting all kinds of benefits I never got. We noticed Mercedes and Lexuses coming to the neighborhood on weekends. A woman across the street was having one kid a year for years. People were coming and going, hanging around on the front porch; they didn't seem to be doing anything. Most of the people were black, a lot of Muslims. The women started wearing burkas. They become Muslims when their boyfriends go to prison and convert. There's a mosque a block away now that doesn't look like a mosque. It's just a house."

Donna says her South River Street and nearby South Main and South Franklin streets are known as Wilkes-Barre's red-light district. She describes the comings and goings of hookers and their pimps matter-of-factly. The pimps are mostly white guys who follow their girls around on bikes, she says. One day she was out front trimming her rosebushes when a hooker stopped by and asked if she could smell the flowers. Donna said sure, but then her pimp told the girl to get back to work. Later, she heard the same girl call out to her pimp down the street, "Eric, I made forty dollars!"

Donna sits on her porch and watches these scenes. One day, a dealer and a customer passing each other tried to make a clandestine exchange of contraband right in front of her house, but the dealer kept dropping the drugs and they had to repeat the maneuver several times.

"It was almost funny, but this is our life," Donna says with a sigh of resignation. "Now I have a house that I have mortgaged to the hilt, and I can't leave."

Was there a relationship between her activism and her decision to back Trump?

"Probably. And I liked his whole stance on immigration too. Maybe I'm a racist and I didn't acknowledge it. I didn't think I was. Again, I thought I was the most liberal person in the world until we moved here. But we have two or three overdoses a day in Wilkes-Barre. You see people in Public Square slouched over, looking like zombies. I saw Trump as a law-and-order figure who would help us get our town back, and then the big one—maybe he could bring some jobs."

Hillary Clinton had no appeal for Donna. Many of her customers at the hair salon said they were going to vote for her, but Donna didn't think they were doing so with any enthusiasm. "They just loved Obama. I don't get it."

Donna told people up front that she was going to vote for Trump. She liked to mention that paper she had written about him years before; she said she'd always admired him and she thought he'd outshone his many competitors during the GOP primaries of 2015. So, in January 2016, she changed her registration from Democrat to Republican so she could vote for Trump in the April Pennsylvania primary.

She took her husband to see Trump at the first rally the candidate held in Luzerne County, just before the primary. Jim was impressed and jumped on the Trump train. He'd been a lifelong Democrat and Trump was the first Republican he ever voted for. Donna too.

"The first rally was ninety-eight percent white," she says. "People were introducing themselves and very friendly. I was sitting with two strangers and got to talking with them. At one point, they had to leave for a while and I watched the lady's purse and iPad. I saw people in the front row offer their seats to a disabled lady. Everyone thought it was going to be violent, but it wasn't. I shared some of what I was seeing at the rally on Facebook, and that opened me up to a whole pile of hate."

Four of her friends unfriended her. To avoid any further trouble, she unfriended some family members and a friend because she knew they were all for Hillary and hostile to Trump. She didn't want the negativity.

One of her customers asked her how she planned to vote, and when Donna said "Trump," the customer said, "How *could* you?" A neighbor reacted the same way. Donna was flabbergasted.

"Are you serious? Have you ever heard of neighbors hating each other over a political candidate?"

But Donna was undeterred, and eagerly made plans to attend the second Trump rally at Mohegan Sun Arena in October, just before the election.

That one was more diverse. "At the first rally, most of the people were white working class. The second rally was everything: Oriental, black, Hispanics. Everything. We got there three or four hours before.

"The rallies were wonderful and so uplifting. He actually gave you hope."

On Election Day, Trump lost the precinct Donna worked at in Barney Farms, an affluent section of Wilkes-Barre, where he took only a third of the vote. When she got home she made herself a stiff drink, watched some of the TV coverage, and went to bed, thinking Trump had lost. When she woke up in the morning and learned he had won, she cried with joy.

"I've never felt so strongly about a candidate before."

Kim Woodrosky

KIM

Kim Woodrosky is a flashy, attractive blonde and self-described bigmouth. But she's also a successful real estate investor who owns several apartment buildings in Wilkes-Barre and drives a yellow Corvette; she never bothered to go to college.

Kim was born into a family of Democrats, her father a teamster and her mother a line worker in a textile mill. She voted for Bill Clinton twice, Al Gore, John Kerry, and then Barack Obama in 2008. Dissatisfied with Obama's first term, she sat out the 2012 election, and in 2016 became a Republican in order to vote for Donald Trump.

"The country elected Trump to get out of the Democratic nonsense," says Kim, who dresses stylishly and vapes to help her quit smoking. "I voted for Obama, but it was a lot like they were turning us into a socialized country. I'm single, fifty-five, not married, and don't have a boyfriend. I'm not rich. But all of a sudden, with health care, if you make more than fifty thousand dollars a year, you're considered wealthy. Instead of giving, giving, giving people money so they can get health care, why don't they do what should be done? Get some revisions to NAFTA and get people working. But no, it was, 'Let's give people this, give people that.'"

Frustration with Obamacare was Kim's driving issue: its high cost, its tangled red tape, and the resentment she felt that others earning less money than she was were slotted into the same plan she had.

"I make over fifty thousand dollars. To qualify for the Affordable Care Act, I have to pay seven hundred and seventy-two dollars a month for myself. That same plan is available to someone making thirty-eight thousand for four hundred and thirty-two dollars a month. The girl next door with state health is making thirty-eight thousand a year. I make more money and am productive to have to subsidize her? Everyone in the country making more than fifty thousand dollars is now subsidizing people making less money. Tell me how that's fair. That's like you and me walking into a car dealership and looking at the same new ninety-thousand-dollar Cadillac, and the guy says, 'You can have it for forty-five thousand, not ninety thousand.'"

Then there are the bureaucratic headaches. Every year, Kim says, her Blue Cross plan is automatically canceled, forcing her to reenroll, and when she does, she learns that her plan has changed in various ways. Last year, she found out that a prescription that used to be paid for is no longer covered. "So they wanted four hundred dollars for one prescription, and it took me two hours on the phone trying to straighten it out.

"I think I'm suffering as much as the person without health insurance because my premiums have gone up so much. I'm paying ten thousand dollars a year now. Where does it end? What if I can no longer afford to pay? One more increase and I'll be paying as much as I do for my mortgage, which is ridiculous.

"So Obamacare was the biggest factor for me, and when someone like Hillary Clinton says, 'If you like the way the country has gone for the last eight years, vote for me,' why would I continue?"

Not that she liked Hillary anyway. Kim did want to see a woman become president, true. Just not *that* woman.

"Hillary was cocky. She felt she had it won. Where did the 'deplorable' comment come from? That came back to bite her in the ass, did it not? I think Hillary thought Trump was just a big joke, and that only the uneducated people were going to vote for him. That pissed off a lot of people too. So, if I liked Trump, I'm not only deplorable, I'm uneducated! She did this to herself."

Hillary represented an extension of the Obama presidency, a presidency that Kim had soured on.

"When I voted for Obama in 2008, I thought the racial issues in America would get better because we were electing a black man. But he made things far worse. Every time a white cop hit a black guy, instead of defending the police department, he went the other way and defended the minority kid. Then we would learn the shooter had a long rap sheet and the cop was just doing his job. I was infuriated with how [Obama] handled the police shootings. He should have stood up and said, 'Enough is enough.' The racial divide grew worse. Minorities took it as carte blanche because they heard nothing from Obama, so they kept running wild. He never put his foot down in the beginning.

"Wait. Before you think I'm racist," Kim adds, "my brother is married to a multiracial girl. So I'm not a racist."

Kim and her younger brother, Shon, forty-five, were born and raised in Wilkes-Barre. Their father, John Woodrosky, was a truck driver, and their mother, Michaelene, was happy to quit her job in the textile mills after she got married. John was a hard-core Democrat but admitted to Kim that he voted for Trump in 2016. Michaelene voted for Hillary and hates Trump. "She said, 'I hated him twenty years ago when he was on TV, and now he's even more obnoxious!'" Kim says, laughing.

She was raised in a friendly neighborhood in the North End of Wilkes-Barre dominated by Polish and Lithuanian families. "It was great back then," Kim remembers. "Your neighbor yelled at you just like your mother did. Everyone looked out for one another and knew each other. It was a small city environment. People would leave their doors unlocked. Those were the days of still having a milkman coming. You could leave money in your mailbox without worrying about anyone taking it."

Kim went to Coughlin High School and pursued a vocational program, studying radio and television. "I wanted to be a TV personality. Not the weather girl, but I envisioned myself to be the blonde Connie Chung!"

Kim passed on college, and after initially training to become a flight attendant at a travel school in Pittsburgh, she had a change of heart and dropped out. After she returned home, her father told her in no uncertain terms that she had to get a job. She waitressed at a Holiday Inn before eventually managing a high-end Italian restaurant for seventeen years in Dallas, an upscale suburb outside Wilkes-Barre. She was in charge of staff in "the front of the house."

During that period, Kim also began dabbling in real estate. Growing up, she and her brother lived with their parents in one unit of a four-unit building that her grandmother had given Kim's father. Now Kim started managing the building for her father.

Then the house next door came on the market. Kim bought it and converted it into two units. Next she acquired a third building that had been in a fire, and a fourth—all on North Washington Street in Wilkes-Barre. She eventually bought the building that she and her parents lived in, after they retired to a cabin in nearby Harveys Lake, a borough in northern Luzerne County.

She now owns eight buildings—three by herself and five more with her brother—and manages twenty others. A patron at the restaurant where she used to work had asked her to manage one of his apartment buildings, which led to other work managing more apartments.

Kim says the buildings she bought were bargain fixer-uppers, ranging in price from $20,000 to $50,000. Now she puts their worth at between $100,000 and $125,000 each.

Her brother works as a prison guard, but is also a working partner with Kim in their real estate ventures; he's in charge of maintenance.

Kim either owns or manages a total of sixty-five apartment units. Six of her sixty-five units are Section 8. She charges $600 a month for a one-bedroom, $750 for two, and $795 for three. She says she tolerates some abuse of Section 8 guidelines, like a supposedly single mother with three kids having her boyfriend live with her, but she wishes the government would crack down on this sort of thing. "It upsets me [that] the government can't figure this out, because it's a major problem."

She has evicted tenants and is tough on laggards. She charges a late fee after four days, and will evict tenants if they haven't paid their rent within ten days, though she'll work with a tenant who is having cash flow problems and can make a partial payment.

"We've made a society that's more than willing to be carried by the government," Kim says. "There's an entitlement mind-set to the core: have one more kid, get more food stamps and more money toward my rent. It blows my mind. It's a never-ending cycle. Why wouldn't there be resentment at that? When my Section 8 tenant tells me she has a third kid, I have to hold my tongue, but do I want to? What I'm really thinking is, 'Isn't that fucking great!' I see every day how these people teach their children to stay on the system. 'Don't worry about getting knocked up because you'll get more money. You have two kids instead of one.' That's the problem we need to fight in this country."

She says the economic outlook for Wilkes-Barre is bleak. "We live in a depressed area, so the rental market is nowhere near what it is in a larger city. The average salary here is less than thirty thousand dollars a year. We don't have enough high-paying jobs. Until we get higher-paying jobs, I don't see the area changing. Young people are leaving. Real estate values are stagnating at best. You can get cheap housing here, but most people can only find ten-dollar-an-hour jobs. I see the financials of my tenants and no one makes more than forty thousand dollars a year. I make ninety and everyone thinks I'm rich! I'll be lucky to get back what I paid for my buildings, but at least the mortgages will have been paid off by my tenants."

Kim is happy with her Trump vote.

"I think he's doing very good. I like his directness, though I think he should tone it down a bit. There obviously have been things he said that I rolled my eyes at. But it's because he's not a career politician. He shoots off the cuff. He says what he thinks, before he says what he's going to say. But who gives a crap about political correctness anymore? We've been worried about saying and doing the right things and not offending people for too long. Political correctness hasn't gotten us anywhere."

Neither has political experience, Kim believes. "Trump has changed politics for the rest of our lives. He's made it so you don't have to be a governor or senator for ten years or more. Or start out as a mayor. Those days are over. Where did experience get us in the last eight years?"

She admires Trump's business savvy and thinks it can help bring a different sensibility to Washington. "We need a guy who's gonna cut through the shit, who's a businessman. So he went bankrupt a few times. That's what businesses do."

And businessmen shouldn't be forced to release their

taxes—even if they get elected president of the United States, Kim says. "His response there was correct. If he did not pay taxes, he took advantage of the tax code that Congress set up. I'm in business too, and I take advantage of everything I can. Why wouldn't I? I don't want people to see my taxes. It didn't matter. He got elected."

The reason Trump was elected, Kim thinks, is that he made voters feel he understood their problems and their fears. People in Luzerne County and throughout much of America, she believes, really do feel ignored, or as Trump said, forgotten.

"I don't think politicians understand what people are going through. And I don't think Trump really does either, actually. But he said he did, and when you say something, people listen. He put himself in office by saying what people wanted to hear. That's what the Democrats did not do. Bernie Sanders just pumped up millennials by getting them to think they were going to get free college. How in God's name are we going to afford that? Trump told the working class what they wanted to hear. They wanted to hear, 'You're the forgotten ones. You're the ones Washington doesn't care about.' That's when they switched over. He had a better message, and he had much larger crowds than Hillary."

Kim thinks immigration is one of the issues Trump was most attuned to, and in Luzerne County, it was Hazleton, where Hispanic immigration has surged in recent years, that served as a microcosm of white worries. Hazleton is now a majority-minority city, and Kim thinks the city is "ruined" as a result.

"It's going to bankrupt the city, because not enough of

the Hispanic majority is paying taxes. And the crime rate is ridiculous. I'm sorry, but every time you turn on the news, it's Diego Garcia, or whoever, that they're arresting. It's becoming a little Tijuana down there. Hazleton used to be run by the Italian Mafia. Now it's the Spanish Mafia. We're just flipping things!"

Nationally, she thinks the so-called Dreamers should be given enough time to go through the process and get themselves legal, and if they can't do it in that time, they should be deported.

While many friendships have fractured as a result of Trump's election, Kim says she's maintained her close ties with Democratic friends.

"My best friend is the biggest Democrat you'd ever want to meet. Three weeks before the election I told him, 'I don't care what the polls say, I think Trump is going to pull this off.' All these Spanish people, I said they're not going to vote, because they have two choices: not Obama anymore, but an old white lady they don't connect with, and a bigmouth white guy they don't connect with. So they'll stay home, and that's exactly what happened.

"I was shocked the night of the election. I have die-hard Democratic friends, and I was watching the returns. I'm saying to them, 'Look at this! Look at that!'"

After the result was clear, Kim turned to one of her friends and said, "Do you hate me now?"

"No," replied the friend, who, after noting how many attachments had been frayed during the campaign, added, "You're looking at two rational human beings."

Feelings were still raw for a month after the election, but

Kim thinks the partisanship and bitterness in her circle have waned by now.

"This 'He's not *my* president' stuff? What the hell is that? I've never seen anything like it. It's a bunch of babies crying. My friends and I sometimes throw gibes at each other, but if you're not intelligent enough to have a conversation without getting into an argument about Trump, come on! It doesn't mean you can't live with one another, for God's sake. If everyone thought alike, the world would be a boring place."

Tiffany Cloud

TIFFANY

Tiffany Cloud, fifty, is a politically active housewife and one-time advertising executive married to a former Army Special Operations officer who did two tours of duty in Iraq and one in Afghanistan. She proudly refers to her husband as "a warrior." She helps him navigate VA red tape to receive the benefits he is due, works to promote veterans' issues and local Republican candidates, and hosts a weekly public affairs show on her local cable TV station.

Tiffany was originally a Ted Cruz supporter, but when he lost the Republican primary, she quickly hopped on the Trump bandwagon. "This area is dying, and Trump had an electric paddle to make people feel he could bring it back to life," she says. "They hoped Trump will deliver a plan, or *something*, for tomorrow.

"You can argue that Luzerne County gave Trump Pennsylvania, which gave him the presidency. And Luzerne represents red America. When I saw thousands and thousands of people at Trump's rally in blue Wilkes-Barre right before the election, I knew he was going to win. He was the working man's billionaire."

Tiffany was raised in Conyngham—a rural borough in Luzerne County outside Hazleton—the elder of two daughters born to Mike and Carol Drewniak. Mike was an executive for the Topps Company, the gum, candy, and sports card manufacturer. Carol was a former ballet dancer and interior decorator who was elected to the Conyngham Borough Council and ran unsuccessfully for the Pennsylvania house of representatives.

"Conyngham is like a Norman Rockwell town," Tiffany says. "Flags on the front porches, everyone says hello. When I was a kid, Main Street was not paved. We had a lot of parades: on Veterans Day, the Fourth of July, even Halloween. Church was very important. I grew up Catholic. I went to Sunday mass and Sunday school, and then Catholic high school in Hazleton."

She went on to Colgate University, where she majored in economics and religion, with a minor in studio art. She was pragmatic but had a creative side that led her into the advertising business in New York. At twenty-six, Tiffany was named a vice president at the Saatchi & Saatchi agency, which sent her to Australia to work, initially, on breakfast cereal accounts, competing against the likes of Kellogg.

"I loved living in Australia," she remembers. "It was not *Crocodile Dundee.* It was very metropolitan. The people tended not to talk about politics. I don't know if they considered it impolite. At a party, they congregated around the barbie. The pace of life there was slower than in the States. People got to know each other before diving into a business deal."

In 1996, after Australia adopted a mandatory gun-buyback program following a rare mass shooting, Tiffany's agency did the advertising to promote the program. "I remember, as an American coming from Pennsylvania, thinking how bizarre that was. I was big on the Second Amendment and guns were part of my fabric. It seemed strange to me." Hunting is in her blood, and she says she still shoots "a mean crossbow."

Approaching thirty, Tiffany returned to America and moved to Atlanta, where she met and married an executive in the hospitality business. They had a son, who died in infancy of a rare cell disorder, and a daughter. The marriage ended in divorce after seven years, and Tiffany moved back to Conyngham to be near her parents as she raised her daughter.

Three years later, looking for love online, Tiffany met Erik Olson, an Army psychological operations officer who was finishing his second tour of duty in Iraq.

After months of online courtship, meeting him in the flesh back home for the first time was like a movie scene. "He marched up to my front door in full uniform and said, 'Hello, ma'am. My name is Staff Sergeant Erik Olson, and I'm the last of the good men.' He had me at hello, to quote that movie, *Jerry Maguire*. Erik is a good man, and he's been very good to my daughter."

That was May 2010, and after five weeks of actual, rather than virtual, dating, Erik, who was also divorced with one daughter, proposed. Smitten, Tiffany quickly accepted, but she didn't have her man for good yet, because he was on a battle roster to go off for a third tour of combat duty, this time to Afghanistan, in January 2011. They married on November 27, 2010, two months before his mobilization date.

"Psyops was in such high demand that they kept sending him back and back. Opting out was not an option for Erik. He's a warrior. He loved it. Absolutely loved being a soldier.

"He'd gotten hit by enemy fire five times in Iraq over the two tours. He got hit a sixth time in Afghanistan, then he was medically retired. They put him out to pasture, much to his dismay. His last injury was September of 2011. A rocket hit nearby and killed some people. Erik got tossed into a razor wire fence and had to be cut out. He had shrapnel injuries. They flew him to Bagram. He'd been in a remote area of eastern Afghanistan. After finally meeting this guy in my forties, I thought, oh my God, I couldn't see him like that when he comes home. I'd lost a child. I'd experienced loss. You learn the military makes the decisions, not you. War isn't over just when it's over. There's the whole time that's spent adapting to life at home. You spend a lot of time healing, physically and emotionally."

★   ★   ★

Tiffany calls herself a "constitutional conservative," and she thought that rubric best fit Ted Cruz, the Texas senator whom Trump ridiculed in the primaries as "Lyin' Ted."

"Among other things, I admired how deft Cruz was, and is, with language, as well as his masterful ability to articulate any situation, backed up with fact and constitutional law," she says. "Trump's style of communication, conversely, is far more direct and simplistic. He communicates in an everyman sort of way that many find refreshing: the direct opposite of the silver-tongued, mostly talk politician that so many who voted for Trump felt they had endured the last eight years. I still think Ted Cruz would have made a great president, but I admire Trump's tenacity and his frankness, which is unusual in politics. I'm really rooting for Trump to succeed. Hopefully he'll succeed in Luzerne County so I don't feel like I have to leave the area."

Tiffany knew that Trump's directness helped him connect with voters who admired his candid and fresh approach, but the flip side was that the same directness was a constant liability on the campaign trail, since one never knew when he was going to veer off script and attack or offend someone.

"Trump's greatest asset is his direct manner of speaking, and his greatest liability is his direct manner of speaking," Tiffany says.

She couldn't abide Hillary Clinton for most of the reasons enumerated in the standard Republican critique: her careless, if not criminal, handling of classified emails as secretary of state; her failure in Benghazi; her campaign's financing of the so-called Russian dossier against Trump (which Tiffany thought was the real collusion); and the feeling that she was out of touch with regular voters.

"In 1999, preceding her official run for the Senate representing New York, Hillary Clinton announced she was going on a statewide 'listening tour,'" Tiffany recalls. "In 1992, during his bid for president, Bill Clinton famously used the phrase 'I feel your pain.' In using this sort of language, the Clintons masterfully created a public perception: they truly heard the people. The irony? Years later, when Hillary ran for president against Trump, many of the American people did not feel heard. Trump beat Hillary Clinton at her own game."

He also deftly flipped the script on Hillary's "I'm with Her" slogan to "I'm with You," to better cement his ties to the forgotten voter.

Tiffany pushes back on the notion that women who voted for Trump betrayed their gender by not making Hillary the first woman president or that they supported any sort of retreat on women's rights.

"Women who voted for Trump didn't seem to be longing to return to the days of barefoot in the kitchen," she says. "On the contrary, many longed for freedom from big government intrusion and control. Big government has become like an abusive spouse to many women—telling us what to think, how to feel, that it will control our money...and that we should just know our place. Many women voted for Trump because we are sick and tired of being dominated by big government. Women are tired of being treated as 'single issue' voters, something the Democratic Party has done. And plenty of women will likely say Clinton assumed she had our vote, merely because we shared a gender."

After Cruz was eliminated, and since Hillary was never an option, it was a foregone conclusion that Tiffany would vote for Trump. But she got more enthusiastic about that after seeing him at his second rally at Mohegan Sun Arena, just before the election.

"It was one of the most patriotic feelings I've ever had," she recalls. "All red, white, and blue and fired up! The place was packed. It was such a moment in politics. Trump walked in and the crowd went wild. It was electric. The Lee Greenwood song 'Proud to Be an American' was playing. I had chills. The excitement and energy were palpable. Trump has a way of connecting with everyone that feels so relatable, which is interesting, since he's a billionaire . . . I think Trump listens. And he heard the forgotten man and woman.

"We don't have lattes here. We don't have a single Starbucks in Hazleton. We don't have metrosexual men with gel in their hair. We have the guy dressed in camo going into the grocery store. Veterans wear their hats here with pride. We have strong, traditional family values, and parades on Memorial Day are big . . . We're hunters here. We're Second Amendment people."

While Tiffany is still digesting Trump's victory and how he pulled it off, she thinks the following conclusions can be drawn as to why she and others supported him:

He was an antipolitician and businessman; he was the strong leader that people were thirsting for; skyrocketing Obamacare rates drove voters from Hillary to Trump; the Kids for Cash scandal in Luzerne County and people's cynicism about entrenched government corruption made them receptive to Trump's frequent charge that Hillary was corrupt; the economy had virtually cratered in Luzerne, and Trump, with his business savvy, might revive it; Trump would control illegal immigration and curb legal immigration; he would protect Second Amendment rights, while Hillary would have eroded them. "People here still believe guns protect us from a tyrannical government," Tiffany says. She felt that Trump would strengthen the military, which had been downsized too much, and that he would slow the secularization of the nation and allow God back into the culture. "Removing God creates a vacuum filled by evil," she says. There was a nostalgia to bring America back to a more familiar time of yesteryear, as personified by Trump's "Make America Great Again" slogan. Tiffany liked that Trump financed his own campaign and therefore was beholden to no one. He was a successful businessman who was able to leverage his celebrity into brand-name recognition, a brand that suggested success.

Tiffany lives outside Hazleton, where there has been a surge in Hispanic immigration. "Many would argue [Hispanics] have not wanted to be 'fully absorbed' into the American fabric, have not assimilated, unlike previous immigrants, like the Polish or the Italians, who did wish to assimilate," she says. "Locally, there was a frustration with the dramatic rise in drugs, gangs, and violence that came with an element of the Hispanic population. Second, there was the impact on education, with the English as a second language program and the associated drop in educational test scores versus the state average."

"It's not that this area is immigrant-averse," Tiffany says. "The aversion is to unlawfulness and a lack of willingness to assimilate," as compared to the white, European immigrants of yesteryear who followed the law and did want to assimilate.

Another worry for Tiffany is property taxes. "We have so many elderly on fixed incomes in the region, and the people want property tax relief. In Hazleton, the older residents often own homes, so they are the ones paying property taxes for the Hazleton Area School District, which has become overcrowded. Many of the newer immigrants are renters not paying property taxes, thus not helping fund the school costs. It's all being shouldered on property owners, many of whom don't even have kids in school anymore. The renter-versus-homeowner topic related to property taxes is an important one in understanding what's happening, certainly in Hazleton."

THE VETERAN

Erik Olson

Exit polls in the 2016 presidential election showed that nationally, Donald Trump won the votes of veterans by a two-to-one margin over Hillary Clinton, so the 840,000-odd veterans who lived in Pennsylvania represented a key constituency for Trump. The state's veteran population represents the fourth largest concentration in the country, after California, Texas, and Florida.

In some respects, Trump seemed an unlikely candidate to attract veteran support. He had never served in the military, having received four draft deferments for attending college and one during the Vietnam War for bone spurs in his feet. He'd remarked that Senator John McCain was not a war hero because he'd been captured as a prisoner of war in

Vietnam. He'd attacked the gold star parents of Captain Humayun Khan, a soldier who was killed in Iraq, after Khan's father criticized Trump in a speech at the Democratic National Convention. And national security experts who served in both Republican and Democratic administrations had declared during the campaign that Trump was unfit to be president.

But as Bill Clinton and Barack Obama had proved, military service was no longer a prerequisite for high office, and Trump staked out positions that were popular with veterans tired of fighting seemingly endless wars in places like Iraq and Afghanistan. His America First doctrine seemed to make prolonged foreign entanglements less likely, and he promised there would be no exercises in nation building. And while Trump criticized George W. Bush for having gotten the country into Iraq in the first place, he condemned Obama for pulling troops out too quickly, thereby creating a vacuum exploited by ISIS, which he vowed to destroy. When fighting was necessary, Trump, unlike Obama, would give a free hand to his generals and support less restrictive rules of engagement—in other words, he would let the troops fight, and not worry too much about civilian casualties, and he would increase the military's budget. Finally, he had talked frequently on the campaign trail about the need to improve services at home for veterans, who had been plagued for years by long wait times for medical attention and tangled red tape for other services.

When the campaign began, Tiffany Cloud's husband, Erik Olson—a seventeen-year Army veteran—didn't see himself as an automatic Trump voter. He was a registered Republican, but there were other candidates in the large GOP field whom he was considering, like Ted Cruz and Carly Fiorina. He was open to considering a Democrat, but not Hillary Clinton.

"I never felt the connection to her in any fashion," says Erik, who is fifty. "I try to think of myself as middle-of-the-road politically and give everyone a chance. I didn't feel a connection to Hillary. Didn't like some of her scandals, if you will. I was blown away by Benghazi, for example. For someone who was going to be commander in chief, I felt she abandoned our guys. Then there were older scandals going back to Whitewater, for God's sake, and I felt no one should be entitled to the presidency, and I thought that's how she was coming across."

But before he could even think about politics, Erik had to recover from the six traumatic brain injuries he had suffered from IED explosions in Iraq and Afghanistan, as well as internal injuries and back injuries from the wear and tear of combat.

Veterans' issues would have been important to Tiffany anyway, but now she had a personal stake in the process, so she immersed herself in the VA's infamous bureaucratic thicket in order to help guide Erik through the complex process of getting his disability benefits. It took two years, until 2014, for the VA to assign him a temporary disability rating and fix a dollar amount that he would be paid for his injuries—temporarily. He would then have to wait several more years to get a permanent rating, or a final dollar amount he would be paid for the rest of his life. Doctors wanted to see if he got better or worse. If he got better, he'd be paid less. If he got worse, he'd be paid more.

Meanwhile, Erik just felt lucky to be alive.

"I still have issues, but I'm doing really well compared to a lot of other guys," he says. "I still have my fingers and toes. I have issues with memory. You can feel the difference in your body after several concussions. When you're in an explosion, the shock wave is what hits you, and your brain kind of rattles around inside your head, in its own brain liquid. It's different from what a football player might get. They're still researching and don't know what the long-term effects will be with TBI, or traumatic brain injury."

After Erik's last injury, during a rocket attack in eastern Afghanistan near the Pakistani border, it was a given that since he'd had so many previous injuries he wasn't going to be sent back to the front lines again.

"So they put me out to pasture, so to speak. I went from the front lines to the rear, from the tactical level to the strategic level, and that was a hard adjustment to make. Once you've experienced combat, there is no greater drug in the world. And once you become addicted to it, and feel the camaraderie, that's something you never want to leave. And to have such a dramatic shift in responsibility—I did not want to get out, personally, but I knew as I went along it was probably the right thing. I had children, I had a wife. I had so many close calls, you go, 'Wow, I'm lucky to be here, so I'm not going to fight the process.'"

Born in Miami, the oldest of three children, Erik's parents were both civil engineers. He was raised in Florida and later south Georgia. In 1986, just before he was due to graduate from high school, Erik obtained special permission from his parents to enlist in the Army at seventeen.

"I'd always wanted to go into the Army since I was a kid," he explains. "It was just the excitement and adventure of the military. I couldn't wait to go in. It was not one of my smarter decisions in life. But you're young and dumb, and that's what happens."

For the next four years he was stationed in Germany, where it was the end of the Cold War and he had a close perch for momentous events like the collapse of the Berlin Wall, the revolutions in Eastern Europe, and the start of the dissolution of the Soviet Union. Erik was a cavalry scout, doing reconnaissance from a base outside Frankfurt. He would be part of patrols, driving hundreds of miles up and down the border separating East and West Germany. They would look across the border from higher ground and watch the Soviets and East Germans peering back at them. "We always assumed the Russians and East Germans were going to invade the West."

Returning home in 1990, Erik stayed in the National Guard for another four years, and then quit the service to take a job in the Cayman Islands importing food supplies for hotels and restaurants. He stayed until 2004.

The seminal 9/11 catastrophe in 2001 gnawed at Erik and made him think about reenlisting. "I wanted to do something from the day it happened to make a difference. But I didn't actually go back until 2005. I was older, had a life, and it was going to be a radical change to reenlist."

The Army asked him to consider its psychological operations unit, or psyops, which is part of the military's Special Operations Forces. He did months of training to learn advanced combat skills, and also what he called advanced military marketing—or how to deal with foreign governments and local tribal leaders. This was about the winning of hearts and minds on the ground, how to woo a potential enemy to come over to the American side, and how to best advance U.S. objectives. Erik went through extensive foreign language and cultural training. By then he knew he was going to Iraq so he learned Arabic, and later Pashto, when he went to Afghanistan.

"If Erik had not been injured again, he'd still be in the service," says Tiffany. "It's not that he loved war. He enjoyed the process of feeling like he was making a difference and doing something important—having a great amount of responsibility for himself and others. Psyops was a very strategic thing in the military. He enjoyed adrenaline and strategy. He loved what he did, and thrived at it."

Tiffany Cloud and Erik Olson

On his return home, Erik had the usual difficulties that combat veterans do in reacclimating to civilian life, but he was pleasantly surprised by the esteem in which veterans like him are held in American society today.

"I think it's night and day from the Vietnam era," he says. "Veterans of my generation, we are thanked for our service on a regular basis, whereas the Vietnam guys were not. I think the nation in general was disgusted with itself for how it treated Vietnam vets. Hippies, so to speak—I'm not saying they were wrong to protest, but they may have realized that placing their protests on the soldiers was wrong. These were mostly draftees that served their country. I think the protesters and the nation in general came to that realization. The counterculture groups, as they got older, realized that some of their anger was misplaced.

"The other side of the coin, though, is that a good part of the population today doesn't even know a veteran who has served, since less than one percent have fought in Iraq and Afghanistan since 2001. So, most families are not affected the way they were when there was a draft and most everyone had skin in the game. Sometimes people look at Iraq and Afghanistan vets as if we're animals in the zoo: they want to pet us, but they don't know what to say. The average citizen for the most part doesn't have a clue about what we went through, so that makes our reentry more difficult."

He vacillates on whether the current all-volunteer Army is the right policy or not. "When I was in combat, I always wanted to see someone who wanted to be there, rather than someone who did not. But I guarantee you that if there was a draft, politicians would be more reluctant to commit us to wars. At the same time, our military is more professional now than it has been in history. The reenlistment rate is very high."

So is the suicide rate for returning veterans, at more than twenty per *day,* a staggering statistic that worries Erik.

"The problem is really unbelievable—an epidemic, really, and it doesn't have to occur," he says. "What happens for a lot of guys with PTSD is they isolate from the local population and areas that cause them stress, like crowds at supermarkets or shopping malls. They go to their basement and don't want to leave. Or they self-medicate by hitting the bottle hard. Depression and despair set in."

To help deal with the suicide problem, and to help veterans (and himself) heal the scars of war, Erik, with Tiffany's help, has launched a TV show called *Warrior Summit Outdoors,* which appears on the Youtoo America cable network. The show, which started in 2014, airs once a week for thirteen weeks, and then the season replays. It is now seen by thirty-five million people, according to Tiffany, who serves as the show's executive producer and writer.

"The average show is hunting, fishing, and off-roading," she says. "They don't talk about their war stories. It's about enjoying camaraderie with fellow combat veterans, almost without words needing to be spoken. Once, Erik brought in a guy who'd gone to Benghazi and was portrayed in the *13 Hours* movie. There's no script. They just talk. Erik wanted to not only help himself heal but help others. He's still serving in that sense, of helping others cope."

Luzerne County and Erik and Tiffany's borough of Conyngham were especially hospitable to vets, and they eased his passage home. The shabby treatment of veterans at the VAs had emerged as a significant issue in the presidential campaign, and it resonated in Luzerne, with its abundance of VFWs and Legion halls, its patch towns where Memorial Day and Veterans Day parades are fixtures, and its flags flying at thousands of houses all year round.

Erik found that he liked Trump's pitch to improve services for vets, as well as what he was saying on other issues. So Erik started to lean toward supporting him.

"I began to drift in his direction. He's a little crass sometimes, which was different than what people were used to, but overall, I liked what I was hearing. I think it was because he was different. He spoke about ending military sequestration, of getting more funding, of giving us new rules of engagement for Iraq and Afghanistan, and getting to the point where our sacrifices were worth it. Getting to complete the mission is the easiest way to look at it.

"I feel we pulled out of our commitments too early under Obama. That was a painful day when I saw that last tank leave Iraq. We had Al Qaeda and the insurgent groups in Iraq—we had them beaten. But instead, we created fertile ground for ISIS to regroup. On Afghanistan, our job is to fix it. To finish it. Just leaving and putting an end date on there was a huge mistake. Our commitment has to be mission-dependent."

With Trump, Erik thought, the question became more about formulating the right policy and deciding how he was going to carry it out.

"You can't be 'Rah-rah America, and we're gonna go kick butt,' because anybody who's seen combat doesn't want the next generation to see combat. So you look at what the candidate will do to support veterans, what's going to be our mission, and if we are going to get into a conflict, what is the reason and what is our exit strategy. The one thing Trump said he would do is listen to his commanders on the ground and listen to their advice. The fight against ISIS was vital, and Iraq was going down hard, but the way they've been fighting the last year is impeccable."

Trump's "Make America Great Again" slogan was also meaningful to Erik. "I felt our nation was going in a more politically correct direction, a more liberal direction, a lack of family values direction. When I heard that slogan, it harkened back to the past, and you remembered a different time— when you knew your neighbor, bringing us back to international prominence, not apologizing for mistakes we made in the Middle East, and being proud to be Americans, as opposed to not being proud. I felt we'd been sliding in a depressing direction under Obama. I think he was apologizing, and he almost gave the impression he did not like America, apologizing for our exceptionalism, and I never understood why."

THE WHITE NATIONALIST

Steve Smith

STEVE SMITH, A strapping forty-seven-year-old truck driver from Pittston, in Luzerne County, heads the Wilkes-Barre/ Scranton chapter of Keystone United, a statewide "white rights" group.

A former Ku Klux Klansman and skinhead, Smith received national attention in 2012 when he was elected to the Luzerne County Republican Committee, thereby vaulting from the white underground into the local political mainstream. Positions on the county committee are not hotly contested, and Smith won his first election merely by writing himself in on the ballot. But he was reelected to a second four-year term in 2016—despite a spate of adverse publicity, as well as scorn from the local Republican establishment, which views him as toxic.

"With Trump winning by such a large margin in Luzerne County, unfortunately, it is not surprising that Steve Smith, somebody with a long history of violence and activity with well-known racist and neo-Nazi groups, won the local

Republican committee seat," said Heidi Beirich, Intelligence Project director for the Southern Poverty Law Center, which tracks hate groups nationally and has been monitoring Smith for years.

An imposing physical presence, Smith stands six feet tall, weighs three hundred pounds, is bald, and wears a goatee. When characterizing his politics, he prefers the more benign term "white nationalist" to "white supremacist."

"I'm white, and I love my nation," he says. "But we don't have borders now, and if you don't have borders, you don't have a country."

Smith—who in 2003 was imprisoned for two months for yelling racial slurs at a black man and throwing a brick at him—is thrilled by the election of Donald Trump, whom he went door-to-door for during the campaign. He thinks Trump's election can be viewed as a so-called whitelash, and that it's been a godsend for the white nationalist message.

"I think Trump has created a climate for us to succeed, because he is saying things publicly that people had only said privately," Smith says. "Donald Trump in 2016 defeated two political dynasties: the Clintons and the Bushes. Trump might change politics as we know it . . . his significance for white advocates was that for the first time in a long time, there was a major presidential candidate in the general election that had a spine. He was accused of being a 'racist' at the start of his campaign and instead of groveling like most politicians do, he stood his ground."

The Southern Poverty Law Center thinks Trump is largely responsible for the number of hate groups in the United States rising significantly in 2017, driven by a surge of membership in neo-Nazi and anti-Muslim groups. The number of neo-Nazi groups spiked from ninety-nine in 2016 to 121 in 2017. Meanwhile, the center recorded 114 anti-Muslim groups nationwide last year, more than three times as many as the thirty-four that were identified in 2015. In all, the center counted 954 hate groups in the United States last year, up from 917 in 2016, 892 in 2015, and 784 in 2014.[1]

"President Trump in 2017 reflected what white supremacist groups want to see: a country where racism is sanctioned by the highest office, immigrants are given the boot and Muslims banned," said Beirich, in releasing the SPLC's annual survey of hate groups in February 2018. "When you consider that only days into 2018, Trump called African countries 'shitholes,' it's clear he's not changing his tune. And that's music to the ears of white supremacists.

"It was a year that saw the 'alt-right,' the latest incarnation of white supremacy, break through the fire wall that for decades kept overt racists largely out of the political and media mainstream."[2]

Trump appointed alt-right guru Steve Bannon, head of the archconservative website Breitbart News, as one of his top White House advisers. Bannon later lost both perches after he emerged as the chief source for author Michael Wolff's tell-all book, *Fire and Fury,* the damning insider account of the Trump administration's first year.

Moreover, white supremacists were electrified by Trump's policy agenda of ramping up illegal immigrant deportations, trying to ban immigrants from certain Muslim countries from coming to the United States, and rolling back civil rights enforcement. Perhaps most notably, they were energized by his not seriously condemning 2017's Charlottesville, Virginia, rally of white supremacists, the largest such gathering in a decade. Former Ku Klux Klan Grand Wizard David Duke called Charlottesville a "turning point" and said that white supremacists intended to "fulfill the promises of Donald Trump" to "take our country back."[3]

At a time of identity politics, the words "white identity" are daring to be spoken more often in the era of Trump, who in large part forged his political prominence within the Republican Party by championing the birther movement that challenged President Obama's U.S. citizenship and by freely injecting racial themes into his campaign.

That was certainly noted in Pennsylvania, which now has the fifth highest number of hate groups in the country, according to the SPLC. Police have also reported KKK leafleting and other activity in Wilkes-Barre and Luzerne County in recent years.

In 2015, about a dozen robed Klansmen burned a twenty-four-foot-high cross on private property in Mountain Top, a prosperous suburb of Wilkes-Barre. The men were members of the East Coast Knights of the True Invisible Empire. "We're called the Invisible Empire because nobody knows who we are," one of the Klansmen, Joe Mulligan, told Wilkes-Barre's *Times Leader* newspaper. "We could be your neighbor. We could be your coworker."[4]

Local leaders, noting that President Obama carried the county twice, deny that the strong Trump vote in the county reflects any significant racist sentiment, but some concede that it remains a latent problem.

"White extremism is mostly under the radar here," says

state representative Eddie Pashinski, a Democrat who has represented Luzerne County in the legislature for twenty-five years.

Steve Smith was an only child, raised by his mother in Downingtown, a predominantly white, working-class borough some thirty miles west of Philadelphia. His father left home when Steve was young, and they have had no contact since. "He didn't care to come see me, so why would I waste my time to come see him?" His mother worked in a factory that manufactured paper products.

Steve began dabbling in racist groups while in high school. He felt frustrated that he couldn't drive safely through neighboring Coatesville, which is largely black, at night. That, along with changing demographics and rising crime, drove him to the Klan. "Back then, the KKK was the only group sticking up for white people. So, I joined the Klan." He was nineteen, and "more radical then" than he is now.

"I saw double standards," Smith says. "I saw racial differences. Blacks seemed to be getting special treatment. There was more criminality in the black community. The lyrics in their music were violent. They were misogynistic toward women. They seemed to have a different culture. It seems whenever you get a high black population, you get more crime and illegitimacy, and poverty. White people knew not to go into Coatesville, and to stay away from there. I thought the KKK were the only ones standing up for white people, for better or worse. I'm older and wiser now and see that the Klan is not the way to go. You do dumb things when you're young, that's all. I'm never gonna regret it, because you learn from your mistakes. I was being rebellious. I think I was look-ing for a thrill as much as I was buying into the ideology of the Klan."

Smith enlisted in the Army in 1990, several months after graduating from high school and participating in Klan marches in Reading, Pennsylvania. He served for five years, including three years in Germany.

He says that in the Army he met other soldiers who were Klan members or white nationalists, and that being in the service only reinforced his racial views. "I met a lot of rural white guys who said the first time they met blacks was when they were in the Army. In Germany, a guy from Montana told me he was never prejudiced until he joined the military. I thought that was revealing. People saw groups of blacks to-gether and saw the way they act. They've got a different view."

While stationed at Fort Polk in Louisiana in 1992, after Klan leader David Duke had run for governor of the state, Smith joined Duke's National Association for the Advance-ment of White People, or the NAAWP, a play on the estab-lished NAACP acronym. Smith admired Duke for trying to take the hard edges off the Klan and make white nationalism more mainstream.

"Duke was smooth and had the right approach," Smith says. "You only alienate people when you dress up in robes and all those silly costumes." The Klan has become a shell of its for-mer self and less and less relevant anyway, he thinks. "Truth be told, a lot of kooks are in the Klan."

In fact, Klan groups declined nationally from 130 in 2016 to 72 last year, the SPLC reported in its annual survey. "The decline is a clear indication that the new generation of white supremacists is rejecting the Klan's hoods and robes for the hipper image of the more loosely organized alt-right movement," the survey said.

In 1994, while still in the Army, Smith was charged with disobeying a regulation that forbids soldiers from recruiting for "extremist" organizations, in his case the NAAWP.

"I was livid!" he wrote in a March 2018 Facebook post titled "The White Soldier's Burden." "The hypocrisy of the allegation was apparent. The NAACP is allowed to recruit members and hold meetings on Army posts. But I was deemed a rule breaker for recruiting for the NAAWP. I was able to beat the preposterous charge with help from my JAG attorney. Though I was finally exonerated, my family suffered months of stress stemming from the prejudicial action brought against me."

Smith wrote in his post that during his five years in the Army, "I observed enough anti-white bias and racial double standards to write a book on anti-white racial discrimination...Whites face discrimination in today's military and expulsion if they use their 'right to free speech' for a pro-white cause. Blacks constitute a sizable percentage of the U.S. Armed Forces, and affirmative action programs help promote underqualified blacks into leadership positions. Many nonwhite sergeants and officers use their positions to discriminate against white men and women in all branches of the military...When American soldiers are inducted, they swear an oath to support and defend America and the U.S. Constitution. But it seems the Constitution no longer applies to racially aware whites. In fact, soldiers who display any white pride or independent thought, or who question white racial subjugation, are methodically drummed out of today's military."

After being discharged from the Army in 1996, Smith returned home to Downingtown and worked for about four years at the factory where his mother was employed, and then for a time as a machinist manufacturing high-pressure hoses before turning to truck driving. He works ten-hour shifts, mostly on hauls from Pennsylvania to New Jersey. He's divorced and has an eleven-year-old son.

Following the service, Smith immersed himself in various white nationalist groups—first the European-American Unity and Rights Organization (EURO), which Duke founded in 2000. After a stint in EURO, Smith joined the neo-Nazi group Aryan Nations in 2002 for six months before quitting. "That was one of the worst groups," he says now. "People in that group were wack jobs."

Then, in 2003, he joined Keystone State Skinheads, or KSS. That was the year Smith and two other KSS members were arrested in Scranton for yelling racial slurs at a black man and throwing a brick at him.

"I was pretty drunk that night," Smith recalls. "I was with two other guys. We ended up in Scranton. One of the guys got out of the car and chased a black drug dealer. He called the police and we got arrested. I refused to testify against my friends. On my lawyer's advice, I pleaded guilty to assault and ethnic intimidation and got two months in prison. The news made a big deal out of it and called it a hate crime. Nothing happened! I can see if he was beaten badly or something. But he was just yelled at by some drunken idiots." Smith says he was not involved in throwing the brick.

In 2008, Smith moved to Pittston, in Luzerne County, and at the same time, KSS changed its name to the milder Keystone United because the word "skinheads" had drawn too much negative attention. The group meets monthly.

"The mission of Keystone United is to remove the guilt we have been taught in the schools to have as white people," Smith says. "We are a white advocacy organization. People are pushing the narrative that whites are evil, and they don't emphasize all the things that we did for the country. A lot of people agree with me. They're just afraid to say it publicly."

Keystone United made sure its members were well represented at Trump rallies throughout Pennsylvania during the 2016 campaign. It also sold "White Lives Matter" bumper stickers, which would sometimes be found in various communities pasted onto street signs or newspaper dispensers.[5]

Around 2010, Smith became the Pennsylvania chairman of American Third Position (A3P), a white nationalist political party that aims to deport immigrants and return the United States to white rule. He tried to recruit members from Tea Party groups, such as one in Scranton, in October 2010, when he said in a press release on A3P's website, "We provided them with a true alternative to the typical dead-end conservatism with which so many of these concerned and partially awakened Americans are involved."[6]

In 2011, Smith founded another group: the European American Action Coalition, which says on its website that it "advocates on behalf of white Americans" in Pennsylvania. He said he wanted a "fresh start" with a group he could launch himself. But today Smith says he's no longer active in the European American group and is only associated with Keystone. He also says he no longer identifies as a skinhead.

Asked if he thinks Pennsylvania, the Keystone State, is fertile territory for the white nationalist message, Smith replies, "Anywhere there's white people is fertile ground."

Smith is working diligently to make his pitch more palatable to a broader audience, and to that end, he has received considerable local news coverage.

In 2008, he and a couple dozen of his followers crashed an NAACP meeting at Wilkes University, in Wilkes-Barre, that had been called to protest the rise of hate groups in the area. "I took about twenty-five guys with me," Smith recalls. "They had called an anti-hate meeting in response to the Klan putting flyers around Wilkes-Barre. We asked to speak at the meeting but they said no. So, we went and waited for the question-and-answer session. We were respectful. I asked the first question. I asked them why they only push diversity in white areas, but not black areas."

In a January 2012 letter to the editor published in the *Times Leader,* Smith wrote, "Many experts predict that, if current trends continue, whites will be a minority in the United States by 2050 . . . If this prediction comes true, it will be catastrophic to our country and well-being."[7]

Three months later, Smith went more mainstream. While voting in the April 24 Pennsylvania primary election, he decided on a whim to write himself in for a position on the Luzerne County Republican Committee. No candidate was named on the ballot for Pittston's fourth ward, and Smith was legally entitled to write himself in and serve a four-year term, as long as he had been a registered Republican for the previous two years, which he had. Delighted with his own mischief, Smith himself announced the news of his election on a website called White News Now and posted a photo of his election certificate.

Horrified local Republicans tried to distance themselves from Smith, and began researching election laws to see if they could expel him, given his racist views and criminal record. Terry Casey, then county chairman, issued a statement denouncing Smith's "abhorrent views," but said the committee's bylaws did not permit expelling a member for his beliefs.

Smith scoffed at the expulsion talk to a reporter at the time. "That's against the Constitution," he said. "That's against free speech."[8]

Smith didn't let his new position deter him from continuing to be a local spokesman for the white nationalist cause. In 2015, after the Klan passed out leaflets in Swoyersville, a borough in Luzerne County, and the mayor there held an anti-hate rally that attracted about a hundred people, Smith showed up and told a reporter covering the event that the crowd's concerns were misplaced. "They should be worrying about the gangs in Wilkes-Barre, not the KKK in Swoyersville," Smith said.[9]

Smith always attended the Republican county committee meetings, which are held monthly, and kept his head down, earning praise from some of his colleagues.

"I will say I had no issue with how he served on the committee," says James O'Meara, who was the chairman of Smith's district after he began serving in 2012. "He did everything correctly. Never got out of line. He was very soft-spoken. He never spoke about his white nationalism during meetings."

Adds Lynette Villano, who was vice chairman of the county committee at the time, "We weren't happy with the kind of publicity Steve was bringing, but we couldn't remove him. He's one of three hundred on the committee overall. He doesn't have any power. He seems like a regular guy. I never heard him say anything racist."

In April 2016, Smith ran for reelection and won handily. Smith shared the news himself on Stormfront, the leading white supremacist online forum and the first major hate site on the Internet. "I won reelection to my position as a Republican committeeman in a landslide!" he wrote. "I got sixty-nine votes out of seventy-three that were cast."

Smith's reelection came on the same day as Donald Trump's resounding win in the Pennsylvania primary, in which he won 57 percent of the vote statewide and 77 percent in Luzerne County. Smith told a reporter at the time that he had voted for Trump and attended his rally at the Mohegan Sun Arena outside Wilkes-Barre the night before. "It was quite the spectacle," Smith said. "It was like going to a rock concert. That place was packed."[10] Smith also went to the second Trump rally in Wilkes-Barre, in October, several weeks before the election.

Unbeknownst to the rest of the Luzerne County Republican Committee, Smith told me that he has recruited five to ten of his followers (he wouldn't name them or specify how many) to run for seats on the committee, and they have all been quietly elected, in a further attempt to mainstream the white nationalist message in Luzerne. But unlike Smith, his cohorts, some of whom are also members of Keystone United, have kept their racist views to themselves and have not yet come out to the voters or to their Republican colleagues.

"I said in 2012, after I joined the committee, that we've got to get involved in local politics, because it all starts local," Smith says. "You have to get involved in your town if you want to effect change."

He says it was hard to recruit people to run because they're basically apathetic, but he's found that saying the words "white community" has become more acceptable now, with the election of Trump. He says even some members of the Luzerne County Republican Committee had pulled him aside and privately told him they agree with what he's saying, but they couldn't say so publicly.

One of the most eventful moments in Trump's presidency to date was right in Smith's wheelhouse: the white nationalists' march on Charlottesville, which erupted in violence when the marchers clashed with protesters. The protesters included a collection of anti-fascist groups known as Antifa, as well as Black Lives Matter supporters. Trump condemned both sides at first, then, under pressure, blamed just the white nationalists, and then finally retook his original position of blaming both sides. Smith says that Trump should have blamed just Antifa and Black Lives Matter, since he alleged that they were the ones who started the violence. Or at least Trump should have maintained his original position of calling out each side, rather than vacillating.

But Smith was far more animated and agitated about press coverage of the event than he was about Trump's handling of it.

"The media narrative that the white nationalists are to blame for the violence is totally false," he says. "It was Antifa and Black Lives Matter that were responsible. The Charlottesville police and the city leaders are complicit in this. The marchers had a permit. They showed up, and a bunch of Antifa and Black Lives Matter were there attacking them. But you read the media narrative and you'd think it was white nationalists. This infuriates me. Charlottesville was fake news. Reporters should just report the news, not push their own agenda."

Smith believes that fighting to preserve Confederate landmarks like the Robert E. Lee statue in Charlottesville is a worthy cause. "It's part of our history. Our Founding Fathers were essentially white nationalists. These protesters are trying to replace us. They're trying to get rid of white people. That's probably why Trump won the presidency."

Smith says it's unfair for critics to dwell on his Klan connection from thirty years ago. "You grow up and you get wiser. Everybody makes mistakes. I refuse to let my past prevent me from speaking out. I earned the right to do that. I served in the Army." He reminds people of that by occasionally wearing his "Veterans for Trump" T-shirt.

"You can't say you stand up for white rights today, though more are starting to, now that Trump is president."

Smith says that he thought race was a big factor in the election and that the Left is overplaying its hand "with this talk of 'white privilege' and trying to shut down free speech at places like Berkeley. People are getting tired of it.

"Someone put flyers out recently saying it's 'okay to be white,'" he adds, referring to material distributed on college campuses and in cities around the country in November 2017. "No organization was named or anything. And it was played as big news. People are seeing through this. The fact that Donald Trump won with the media calling him racist proved to me that people are pissed off and that's why he won."

184

THE CHRISTIAN

Jessica Harker

THOUGH LUZERNE COUNTY is predominantly Catholic, there is a significant and growing evangelical community. Nationwide, evangelicals went 80 percent for Donald Trump in the election and made up nearly half of his total vote.

One of Trump's most ardent Christian followers is Jessica Harker, a sixty-year-old registered nurse who works for the Wilkes-Barre VA Medical Center on the four-to-midnight shift. She grew up in Michigan and moved to Wilkes-Barre in the mid-1980s. Later, she married Ray Harker, a born-again conservative Republican active in local politics. He served as both her religious and political mentor, introducing her to God and the GOP.

In the 2016 election, Jess went all-in for Trump, despite the fact that Ray thinks the president is a satanic fraud, and they have spirited arguments about him. She describes their house now as a "no-fly zone."

But she was with Trump from day one, and believes God chose him to end America's political dysfunction. She's been involved in politics for some time and played a role in Lou Barletta's election to Congress. She prayed often for Barletta, as she did for Trump in 2016, and does to this day. During the campaign, she dismissed Trump's history as a womanizer and his crudeness, saying, "We're all sinners." She says the country needed a president who has Trump's "balls."

Jess was the third of four girls born to Chester and Gloria Kaminski in suburban Detroit. Chester was a Ford supervisor and two of his brothers also worked for Ford—as did Jess's grandfather and two uncles on her mother's side. It was a Ford, pro-union, Catholic, and Democratic household.

"Everyone worked for Ford," Jess says, and there wasn't any discussion of politics. "I remember asking my father what the difference between a Democrat and a Republican was, and he said, 'The Democrats are for the working man and the Republicans are for the rich.' That's all."

Chester was Polish and Gloria Italian. His parents had emigrated from Poland and hers from Italy. Jess identifies as Italian.

"I graduated high school in 1976 and the eighties were a blur," she recalls. "My father left the house and my mother was mentally ill. She had to be institutionalized. It became a broken home and I was virtually raised by my Italian grandmother."

188

She followed a boyfriend to Wilkes-Barre in 1985, when she was in her late twenties. She worked at various restaurants and bars, and at Genova Products, a plastics manufacturing plant in Hazleton. She started nursing school in 1993.

In 1996, she met Ray Harker at an AA meeting. Ray had grown up in Luzerne County, went to Temple University in Philadelphia, and then returned home and started a landscaping business. He'd first gone to AA in 1993 to seek help for alcoholism and drug abuse. Three years later, Jess needed help for the same issues.

Ray says that he was agnostic when Christian friends he met at AA led him to a spiritual awakening: "I was led to the Lord and I accepted Christ as my personal savior in February of 1994." He was also a conservative Republican who believed there should be little or no separation between church and state: "The Bible commands that 'everyone must submit himself to the governing authorities,'" he says, quoting from Romans 13:1. "So it stands to reason that we need to ask: To what type of government do we want to submit?" Ray wanted to "reverse the trend of ungodliness that has taken over in our society and government."

While courting Jess, Ray began to teach her about religion and politics and the nexus between the two. She was taken by this charismatic guy, who was two years her junior and talked as if he was a budding pastor.

"Here I was a Democrat from Detroit and a union family, then I met Ray, and he started talking about the Republican Party, and that capitalism is good for our nation," Jess recalls. "He educated me—first about the Lord, then my political beliefs. All I knew was that the Republicans were for the rich and Democrats were for the poor. I was just in my thirties, going to school to be a nurse. I was Catholic. He told me about the saving grace of Jesus Christ. Ray witnessed to me about that."

There was no early revelatory moment. God just reeled her in for a while. "I would call Ray—I'm reading the Bible—and I'd ask him what grace was. Grace is undeserved mercy. Grace is you get to go free. I always thought God was up there taking notes about what I did, and I would never get there. I looked at what the Democrats had been doing and I said, 'This is all wrong.' I told my sisters and they became Republicans. My votes cast my beliefs."

Later, Ray told her about the Founding Fathers and how the Constitution came to be written. She found the story exciting. "Then I was on fire. If our Founding Fathers had not won, they would have been hung. Because who could have known they could beat the British? They were fighting for freedom. They would have been dead if they did not win. I believe that God had plans for America, and that everything which happened to this country was a God thing. Look what we turned into. We have freedom of religion. The Puritans wanted to worship God in the purest form. God took notice of that. The history of the nation is lovely and holy. They're taking that out of the schools because they don't want to talk about religion there. But you can't take God out of government. God *is* government."

Jess and Ray were married in 1997.

She was baptized in 1998 at Conyngham Valley Bible Church, not far from Hazleton. There were about a hundred people there. "It was wonderful. I was making a statement that I was standing for Christ. I realized God was alive and not dead. I'd been fighting against God all these years. I was a Democrat before I met my husband and before I met the Lord. Then I started to see why God wanted me. God may not be a Republican but he darn sure isn't a Democrat! He couldn't be a Democrat because they stand for gay marriage, entitlements, Disability City, abortion, the feminist movement, unions, high taxes, and they're against capitalism."

Ray and Jess both got involved in local politics. Ray worked on Lou Barletta's 2008 campaign for Congress, coordinated the distribution and posting of campaign signs, and helped with fund-raising.

Jess was part of a prayer group boosting Barletta.

"We prayed for Lou. I was driving to work one day and there was this stripper bar. I prayed for it to close and it did! So, I got hooked up with a fellowship group every Wednesday and we would pray, crying out to the Lord for our country."

In 2010, when Barletta was elected to Congress on his third attempt, Ray, with Jess's help, developed a set of a dozen principles called the Core Values of the First District Republican Party of Luzerne County. These values included support for self-reliance and responsibility, a strong military, limited government and low taxes, the right to keep and bear arms, and the notion that private property is necessary for freedom.

That same year, Ray founded God in Government, a teaching ministry designed to educate Christians in political ideology and civic responsibility. He was critical of other Christian leaders who he felt had remained "politically neutral in the culture wars for fear of offending their flocks," he wrote on the group's website. "As a result of such a deliberate omission of the Bible, as it relates to some of the most important areas of life, we have grown inherently liberal in our teaching. Such omission of God's truth for the sake of political correctness and personal ambition is nothing more than a form of deception."

By this time, Ray had sold his landscaping business to start a pest control venture, but in 2014, as God in Government was developing, he decided to sell the pest control business and devote himself full-time to his teaching ministry, whose name he changed to Liberty Lighthouse Ministries. He traveled widely, wrote, lectured, and became a prominent conservative activist.

When the 2016 presidential campaign began, Jess—the former Detroit Democrat who had grown up in a liberal, union household—had become a hard-core, born-again conservative Republican. She couldn't wait for the Obama presidency to end, and she was acutely aware of what she saw as the enormous culture gap that existed between what Democrats, liberals, and much of the media believe and what Middle America believes.

"If you watch what middle-aged to older Americans watch on TV, especially when they're sick, they watch *Mayberry R.F.D., M*A*S*H, Gomer Pyle, Leave It to Beaver,* or the old TNT movies," Jess says. "Things that are not sexually stimulating—just good, old-fashioned 1950s-style TV. Middle America thinks the same way. They like apple pie, the Fourth of July, and Memorial Day. I don't think the Left has any idea what the rest of the country is thinking or talking about. Mainstream Americans won't go out of their way to make their opinions known ... They just love their home and they love their God.

"When the left-wing Democrats thought they could push their agenda on us, Americans just got tired of it. Like, the gay agenda was one thing. But transgender bathrooms? That's a different story. I think you guys, the media, don't realize how apple pie America really is. The liberal Left has an agenda to marginalize the Christian history of this nation. Gay marriage equates to a rapid decline of moral values and encourages the downward spiral of a nation. Gay marriage was rubbing everybody's noses in it. Then the transgender thing. I'm not against gay people, and God looks beyond the sin to the sinner. But gay marriage is just not the natural state of affairs.

"As for the media, when they saw that Trump could win, they started trying to catch him with those gotcha stories. 'Did you hear what he said last night?' But nothing happened because President Trump said what Americans were really thinking. That's what shocked liberals. But it was obvious to the evangelicals what was going on. Everyone knew the media were liberal and they were going to pick and choose what they wanted to present. It's like coloring. If you want to color something some way, you take a bad photo. Evangelicals knew the media. After a while, people saw the bias, and with the bias came the obstructionism. I don't think Congress obstructs as much as the daily newspapers. People are tired of it."

Jess was repulsed by Barack Obama.

"In Obama, Democrats elected a community organizer, a Saul Alinsky radical, and then they wondered how our society has declined," she complains. "It just burns me up when liberals try to sit in the God chair and dish out words like 'moral decline,' when they're the ones polluting the pond. Hollywood is in an epic moral free fall. The universities are tenured with radical, hippie socialists, if not downright communists. The public schools kick God off the premises, if that's even possible. They are rewriting history so that Western civ is no longer taught. And we are in a moral decline? No kidding! Duh."

Under Obama, Jess says, evangelicals were doing a slow boil. They were determined not to allow his agenda to continue into a Clinton administration. She thought Obama disregarded American principles, dishonored the military, and tied its hands with overly strict rules of engagement. "He thought Americans were stupid, and he made a crucial mistake and misjudged their patriotism. So, when the election time was here, people were pissed off!

"As an evangelical Christian, I couldn't even look at Obama. He was such a degradation to the office, how he carried himself nationally. What he did to America was unbelievable. We witnessed our president marginalize our country by bowing down to foreign leaders to degrade American exceptionalism. I am going out of order, but one of the most disturbing moments I remember right off the cuff is Benghazi. That was one of the saddest days in America because an ambassador was treated that way just because it was election time and Obama didn't want to call it a 'terror attack.' And I watched in utter horror as he shoved Obamacare down our throats in closed meetings after he promised that his tenure would be transparent."

After the Supreme Court upheld the right of same-sex couples to marry in 2015, Jess thought it was offensive that Obama ordered the White House lit up in rainbow colors to celebrate. "Mind you, a good part of America was against gay marriage. So instead of understanding the country's divide on this issue, Obama opted to illuminate the exterior of the White House with rainbow colors, which further divided the nation. I liken that to rubbing Judeo-Christian noses in dog dirt, until it stuck to their nose hairs. Then the attempt to put transgender bathrooms in the public school system was like someone saying 'Open your mouth and say "Ah"' while holding a spoonful of human excrement. After all that, was an olive branch extended? Was there any attempt to soothe the hurt that was purposely flung in our faces? *No.* So like they said in *The Godfather,* you go to the mattresses."

She accused Obama of pulling out of Iraq too soon, thereby giving birth to ISIS. "And in our country, he basically kicked off Black Lives Matter by refusing to allow police to enforce the law while people ransacked cities due to feelings of inequality because they didn't have material items that they were too lazy to work for.

"I believe Obama is a Muslim. Yes, I do. I believe he's anti-American. He bowed to people. You don't bow to anyone when you're the United States president. He made America average, not outstanding. That's what Obama's intention was, to apologize for our way of life and what we've done for freedom. We've always fought for freedom, and freedom's never free. I see that every day with people lying in the beds of my VA."

Jess was hardly alone in continuing to believe the canard that Obama was a Muslim. A May 2016 Public Policy survey conducted when Trump was the presumptive Republican nominee for president revealed that only 13 percent of his supporters believed that Obama was a Christian, while 59 percent believed he was not born in the United States—the false charge Trump had championed as a candidate. And Jess wrongly believed that Obama had shunned the annual National Prayer Breakfast, a Christian mainstay, when actually he attended every year he was in office. Obama also started a tradition of hosting Easter breakfasts for Christian leaders across the ideological spectrum, at which he spoke candidly about his Christian faith. Trump, after assuming the presidency, ended the Easter breakfasts.[1]

When the Republican primaries began in 2015, it did not take Ray long to settle on his choice: Senator Ted Cruz of Texas. Cruz was a Southern Baptist with strong evangelical bona fides. He had what Ray thought was a biblical worldview. He was a constitutionalist and a true conservative. As for Trump, Ray thought he was a joke and did not take him seriously at first.

But Jess was intrigued by Trump.

"We had every Tom, Dick, and Harry running in the Republican primaries," she recalls. "It was a media frenzy, and who got the most airtime? President Trump. Trump was very aggressive when he dealt with his Republican opponents. I don't think it was right, but it was effective... He fought dirty, but he was still saying the things that I wanted to hear, and he won. He had balls.

"I couldn't stand Hillary, and it was in the back of my mind, thinking about who could beat her. With all the media coverage Trump was getting, he started to grow on me, and to be honest, I wanted someone fresh and new. I'd had it with conventional politicians up to here. Trump was success-ful, and he wasn't afraid to speak his mind and tell people what he thought. He was passionate about his agenda. 'Make America Great Again' made sense, and immigration was a big deal. Americans had just watched those poor children brought in by freight trains from South America and people said, 'Enough!' It's considered a curse when a nation has an influx of immigrants left unchecked...and it's especially dan-gerous when it's done without due process."

Jess noticed that Trump seemed to brush off any sort of incoming fire he encountered from his opposition, and that he always gave better than he got. "He was 'Teflon Don,' and nothing stuck to him," she says. "Ray would tell me, 'This comment is going to do him in for sure,' but we would wake up, check the news, and nothing. There is a biblical explanation for this, because God himself places rulers on the throne. Whether it's to punish us or bring us back from the edge, God has the supreme vote, and I think he used it. The verse is in Daniel 2:21 and tells us that God is ultimately in control. 'He changes times and seasons; he deposes kings and raises up others. He gives wisdom to the wise and knowledge to the discerning.' I began to believe that President Trump was God's man to be elected and no one was going to stop him."

Ray, meanwhile, was horrified that Trump was starting to gain traction, winning primaries, and, even more surprisingly, gaining endorsements from evangelical leaders.

Ray knew evangelicals would have their biggest impact in weeding out the Republican field in the primaries since, as strong conservatives, they would vote overwhelmingly in the general election for whoever won the Republican nomination. They had been culturally conditioned for decades to shun Democrats. In the primaries, the obvious evangelical options in 2016 were Mike Huckabee, the Christian minister and former Arkansas governor who had run credibly for president in 2008, and Ted Cruz, Ray's choice.

Jessica and Ray Harker

"Trump was a con job as far as I'm concerned," he says. "I lost a lot of friends over this. I saw how many evangelicals were confused about how the Bible influenced their ideology. I think anyone who truly held a biblical worldview would have had to go to Cruz. But pastors don't teach a biblical worldview anymore. They just go by whether he's pro-life. If he is, they'd vote for him. Evangelicals were not discerning enough. I thought there was no way they'd go for Trump, because he was a joke that got out of hand.

"I can't wrap my brain around the fact that men like Jerry Falwell Jr. and Robert Jeffress endorsed Trump right off the bat. I thought we were ideological—Trump is nonideological. He believes the Constitution is antiquated. He sees Congress as his subordinate rather than his equal . . . an impediment to his agenda. He is an authoritarian and a demagogue. Trump is a horrible role model for our congregations. What type of mixed signals are our kids receiving if their parents support and defend such a man as Trump? What are adults in the pews supposed to think of their pastors who are contradicting the Bible each time they justify Trump's words and actions?"

But Jess held her ground against the man who was not only her husband but her political and spiritual guide.

"Ray is superconservative. He was watching Trump and freaking out, but I said, 'I like him.' I said I was for Trump and I didn't care what he thought! I finally stood up to him and said, 'I do not believe that.' I felt I had a voice other than what my husband was saying . . . It took me a lot of time to take a stand against Ray."

She concedes that Trump did make multiple outrageous comments along the way, but she liked his feistiness and thought "the American people were ready for a fight."

One of those outrageous comments came late in the campaign, when news of the *Access Hollywood* tape broke. But Jess thought it was no big deal.

"In my job, I'm on the floor talking to the nurses every day. They say 'A guy's a guy.' I mean *Fifty Shades of Grey* was number one in the country! This guy says something wrong, and it's supposed to be taken literally? I think the American people gave him a pass...He wasn't running for office then. He didn't know he would have a political future."

Jess also considered her Christianity. "Christians don't judge the past in every aspect because 'we all have sinned and fallen short of the glory of the Lord'—Romans 3:23."

And she considered history and realpolitik. "Every president besides George Bush one and two had affairs. This election was not about moral justification. It was about winning."

So Jess made up her mind to proudly vote for Trump.

"I stood in a line for three hours to vote for him. People who I knew were rock-solid Democrats were standing next to me, and they were voting for Trump too. I think people had a sense of urgency. President Trump struck a chord, a note, that everyone could understand. That note was, let's 'Make America Great Again,' not bow down to people.

"People believed in him. He was so illiterate politically that he was genuine. He was not schooled in political correctness. He was just telling people what he thought, and that's what the American people liked, and they believed he could win. America changed her mind on the direction of this country. I think President Obama was inching our way toward mediocrity and taking the greatness away from this land...He was scaling that back, and Americans said no."

Trump was espousing what evangelicals believed in: limiting government, protecting the United States, honoring the military, turning trade and the deficit around. And he spoke to what Jess cared about: the coal industry, the steel industry, and the military; how all the jobs were going overseas; and how Americans were getting the short end of the stick. "He promised to keep us safe and I believed him. He was different than regular politicians in that he wasn't prepped by the party. He stood up when other people sat down. He didn't do this gracefully, but he did it effectively."

She thought the country had prayed to God for guidance in the election, and he had sent them Trump. "People came out in droves to vote for him. We were all being encouraged by God."

When Trump was running, Jess wasn't part of an organized prayer group the way she had been when Lou Barletta ran.

"I'd pray on my own. I prayed Trump would win. I prayed all the time. Every day, every time I saw him, every time I walked past the flag, which is a lot because I work for the VA. God woke me up the other night and told me to pray for Trump on North Korea. I woke up and I had a deep concern...God encouraged me to pray for President Trump a bunch that day. I was doing dishes. And he told me to pray."

How did she know it was God?

"Because I know his voice. It's the softest, sweetest voice I've ever heard. If I'm his daughter, why wouldn't he want to talk to me? I always do a global prayer: 'Please guide and direct President Trump. Help him in his new job, and please surround him with effective leaders who can show him the way to go. Put a stumbling block in front of his enemies, get him through these obstruction debacles, and make him more effective with his word, and his communication tools. Put an angel behind and before him.'"

When Trump won the Republican nomination, Ray actually took a heretical step for an evangelical and came out for Hillary.

"The theory in going for Hillary was maybe we could reboot over the next four years, maybe get it right the next time—not have some goofball like Trump come in and destroy the party. Republicans were drifting left. Reactionary conservatives like me were trying to drag the party to the right. We were fighting the Left. But now our enemy has hijacked our party, and I don't know if we can recover from this. Conservatism is out the window. It's Trumpism. My world is upside down."

Having mentored Jess on religion and politics, Ray is still incredulous that she voted for Trump. "My wife was my top cheerleader. Now we can't even talk about politics."

Today he calls Jess a "Trump bot" and says they are now in counseling over their political differences.

Jess, for her part, says their counselor has advised them to fast from the news and not to talk about anything that relates to Trump.

"My husband comes walking in the door talking about everything that's wrong with Trump, but I believe in Trump!" she says. "He was the underdog and I think he has America's best interests at heart.

"This is a daily drama at my house. Ray comes in and I say, 'No-fly zone!' The little time I have at home with him, I don't want to mix politics with that. That doesn't belong in my living room every day. It's been like World War Three with us."

Despite their media fast, she thinks Ray still watches TV when she's not home. "Rachel Maddow is Ray's favorite now because he hates Trump so much. Rachel Maddow! I mean, I don't even know this man! He's had a psychiatric breakdown because of Trump!"

Assessing Trump's impact on their relationship, Jess says that "'strain' is too pleasant a word to describe what this has done to our marriage. It has torn, ripped at, and tried to squash anything we built. We were, and still can be, in serious trouble if we talk about Trump."

THE CONGRESSMAN
(REPRISE)

Lou Barletta and Trump

LOU BARLETTA ENDORSED Donald Trump for president on March 22, 2016, about a month before the Pennsylvania primary, thereby becoming only the fourth Republican congressman to do so.

"I am discouraged that certain members of the Republican Party have spent more time trying to figure out how to stop Donald Trump than they have trying to understand why he is so popular in the first place," Barletta said then. "Voters are smart. We need to listen to the voters instead of elitists trying to tell us right from wrong."

A grateful Trump named Barletta cochair of his Pennsylvania campaign, along with another Republican congressman from the state, Tom Marino. Barletta and Marino became Trump's key surrogates in Pennsylvania and would serve as his main warm-up act at rallies. Trump randomly called them "Thunder and Lightning." Lou was Thunder.

By October, though Barletta was feeling good about Trump's chances in Pennsylvania, polls had him down by six points in the state, and the candidate had been having a rough month around the country.

The *Access Hollywood* tape had leaked on October 8. More women had then come forward to accuse Trump of kissing or groping them without their permission at various times over the years. In the final presidential debate on October 19, Trump had called Hillary Clinton a "nasty woman," and his performance had generally been panned. On the twentieth, he had been booed at the Al Smith charity roast in New York after attacking Clinton, with whom he shared the dais. And on the twenty-first, speaking in North Carolina, Trump was hoarse and seemed in a funk, saying that if he lost, "what a waste of time" it all would have been.[1]

The following day, Trump wasn't much cheerier as he arrived back in Pennsylvania for what his staff was billing as a major speech in Gettysburg on what he would do in his first one hundred days in office. Barletta met Trump before the candidate was to deliver his remarks in a ballroom of the Eisenhower Hotel and Conference Center in front of about five hundred local Republican activists. Trump handed Barletta his speech to read. Top campaign aides Steve Bannon and Kellyanne Conway and former New York mayor Rudy Giuliani were also part of the candidate's entourage that day.

If, on that hallowed ground, Trump hoped to achieve even some of the heft and unifying gravitas of Lincoln's famed Gettysburg Address, he fell way short. He began with a bitter litany of his own grievances, saying that the system was rigged against him; that there was rampant voter fraud; that Hillary Clinton should not even have been allowed to run for president in the first place, but the FBI and Justice Department had covered up her crimes; that the media was dishonest, corrupt, and biased against him; and that after the election, he would sue each of the women who had falsely accused him of sexual assault.

Trump went on to list dozens of things he wanted to accomplish in his first hundred days as president, including imposing term limits in Congress by amending the Constitution, rescinding every executive order issued by President Obama, and renegotiating the North American Free Trade Agreement.[2]

After the speech, a subdued Trump asked Barletta to come talk with him and Steve Bannon. Trump groused that he was down six points and sliding in the Pennsylvania polls, and he said he was thinking of pulling out of the state to put his resources in other places where he had a better chance to win. What did Lou think?

Barletta was taken aback. "I think that was a pivotal moment. He was serious. He said he was down six and sliding, and maybe we should focus on other states. He said it matter-of-factly. I think he wanted to see my reaction. He always wants to know your opinion. He always made me feel like my opinion mattered."

So Barletta made an impassioned case to fight on in Pennsylvania, not quit.

"I pleaded with him not to pull out and I assured him that the polls were wrong," Barletta says. "I said Hillary would not win the southeastern part of the state around Philadelphia by the same margin as Obama did, and that northeast Pennsylvania was how he was going to win. I said, 'You will win in the northeast by margins you're not going to believe.'"

Barletta says that Bannon later complimented him on his persuasive pitch, and assured him that Trump would not pull out of Pennsylvania.

Barletta's gut had told him Trump would win. "There was no doubt in my mind. I've been around here my whole life. I've never seen anything like it. People say signs don't vote, but it means something when they are in someone's yard. And they were all over the county. I saw signs in Democratic houses that I never saw. Trump just spoke their language. His message resonated. It went right to the heart of people in northeast Pennsylvania. He was speaking to people who had given up, who had lost hope in Washington. *He* was their voice and hope. These are tough people. They're no-nonsense. They want it told the way it is, without any BS.

"When he talked about illegal immigration, that really rang a bell. Also, he wasn't politically correct, and said what he felt. They liked that he said he was going to put America first. They liked that he was using his own money and Washington couldn't buy him. They liked that he said we were getting hammered on trade deals. What I heard most was, 'He's saying what I'm thinking.'"

Another indicator of Trump's strength for Barletta was the level of grassroots organizational support he received. "The media kept saying Trump had no ground game. Let me tell you something: all I had to do was turn on the lights of a campaign office and they came out of the woodwork. This was an organic movement like I'd never seen. The polls were never right. It was so obvious if you were there. People were harassing me for signs, stealing signs out of other people's yards, and coming out to make calls.

"And of course there was the silent vote—the undercover Trumpers. In Pennsylvania, they made you feel that if you supported Trump you were either uneducated or racist, so a lot of people went underground. And you had a lot of Democrats who were not going to tell their mothers they were with Trump, never mind the pollsters. Little did they know their mothers were for Trump too! There was a huge silent vote."

Trump would say something controversial almost daily, so Barletta always had to help put out brush fires.

"The bad days were when he said something and everyone would say, 'Now he's done,' and amazingly, his numbers would go up. Whenever he had bad days, of course the media would turn to me and say, 'What do you say about that? Do you still support him?' I had to deal with that constantly. Of course, I never thought about not supporting him, and it seemed like he got stronger every time a controversy would arise from what he said. But I thought it was just Trump being Trump. I grew up in a big family that was a tough family. Words didn't mean as much as action. People believed that he was going to do what he said he was going to do."

Which was to "Make America Great Again," a potent slogan that struck a chord with the Trump base in different ways. For Barletta, it meant that "no one would push America around any longer. When I was growing up, I thought there was no country like the United States, and no one could ever defeat us. Nobody messed around with America. In time, I feel like we've lost that stature. We've lost respect around the world. Countries came in and took our jobs from us. And we didn't fight back. The slogan brought back what the country should be. We were blessed to be born here and no one has got the right to come in and just take it. It doesn't mean you're not welcome. It's a country of immigrants, but people remember how their ancestors came here: legally. My grandmother, born in Italy, would not let her children speak Italian. They had to learn English."

Barletta said there was an undercurrent of resentment among Trump supporters against people they felt were perfectly capable of working but who chose to draw government assistance instead. "People resent seeing people get things they didn't work for. Most Trump voters were not getting anything from the government and were not asking for anything. But I've watched people sell their Access cards for drugs. I was in a Giant supermarket one day, and there was a woman who must have been at the checkout for fifteen minutes. Poor guy behind her, all he had was a pack of Klondikes, and they were melting as he was waiting. You hate to judge, but the woman was dressed pretty well. When people see that over and over again in a tough area like Luzerne County, they want someone to do something. That person was Trump."

In the final two weeks before the election, Barletta helped stir up crowds by riffing on the phrase "last chance." He was in good form on November 7, the night before the election, when Trump returned to northeast Pennsylvania—this time to Scranton, just up the highway from Wilkes-Barre—for a rally.

Opening for Trump, Lou attacked Hillary for wanting open trade and open borders, wanting to expand Obamacare, and wanting justice for all—just not for her. Then he told the rowdy crowd, "Now listen: America needs an honest leader. America has been craving an honest leader, not a politician. Not someone who will tell you what you want to hear, but will tell you how it is. This is once in a lifetime for us, ladies and gentlemen. It will never happen again. Not in our lifetime will we ever have this chance again…

"This is our last chance to stop Obamacare. This is our last chance to secure the borders and build the wall! This is the last chance to stop illegal immigration so that our children and our country can be free and secure and safe. This is the last chance for the rule of law. This is the last chance to make sure our men and women in the military get everything they need to keep themselves safe and protect our country… And this is our last chance to protect our Second Amendment rights. And this is our last chance to protect the life of the unborn. And this is the last chance that we'll have to say 'Merry Christmas' if we want to say 'Merry Christmas,' and we don't have to apologize to anybody! And this is the last chance we have to drain that swamp! Tomorrow let's elect Donald J. Trump the next president of the United States of America!"

The crowd broke into a chant of "USA! USA! USA!"

The next day, Trump was indeed elected president, and crucially, he won Pennsylvania by just 44,292 votes—out of nearly six million cast—largely on the strength of his showing in Luzerne County. The congressman was proud of that, and he liked to think he played a key role in delivering the state—and perhaps the presidency—to Trump.

The president-elect did not forget. "So, after the election—I still have the voicemail—the president called and said, 'Lou, this is Donald. Boy were you right about Pennsylvania!'" Barletta says, chuckling.

A grateful Trump soon asked Barletta to come to New York to discuss a cabinet position.

"It was secretary of transportation originally," Barletta says. "That's what I was called to Trump Tower to discuss. When I got there, it felt like I was going on *The Apprentice*. I'd seen two news reports: one that I was going to be named transportation secretary, then another that Elaine Chao [former secretary of labor under George W. Bush and Senate Majority leader Mitch McConnell's wife] was going to be named. I went in anyway. It was the president, Vice President Pence, Reince Priebus, Steve Bannon, and General [Michael] Flynn. Pence and Flynn left. Then they talked to me about becoming labor secretary. Transportation had gone to Elaine Chao. Transportation was what I was interested in. I felt I could help more in the House because labor was not my expertise or interest. There was not a formal offer. It was, would I consider labor?"

But Barletta remained a Trump favorite. So when it came time to decide who the Republicans would put up to challenge Bob Casey, the incumbent Democratic senator from Pennsylvania, when Casey vies for a third term this November, the president knew just the man.

"It was pretty funny," Barletta says. "I was in my apartment and the phone rang. The ID came up as an unknown caller, so I didn't answer it. Then a Capitol operator called but I still did not answer it. Then my chief of staff called and said, 'The president is calling. Can you please answer the phone?'"

After the two exchanged pleasantries, the Pennsylvania Senate race came up.

"You would have been good in the administration, but I needed you in the House," Trump said. "Now I need you in the Senate. Announce tomorrow."

"I'll have to think about it," replied the startled Barletta, stalling for time.

"What do you have to think about? If I back you, you'll win."

"Well, I have to talk to my wife about it."

"Well, talk to her and announce tomorrow!"

It was not the next day, but Barletta did eventually announce, and won the Republican Party endorsement in February to face Casey, whose father had served as governor of Pennsylvania for two terms.

Barletta thinks he will need to raise about $25 million to run a viable campaign. He says that Trump has assured him he will both help him raise money and come to Pennsylvania to help him campaign, just as Barletta did for the president.

"The Senate campaign is going well so far," Barletta says. "It's going to be interesting. Casey is a big name. When you think of Pennsylvania politics, you think of the Caseys. But you couldn't contrast two people more than Bob and myself. For a long time, he was a moderate Democrat that seemed to fit well here, but in recent years he's moved very left of center. He was one of the six senators to call on the president to resign. Obviously, with me being a Trump supporter and cochair of his campaign in Pennsylvania, this race will be seen as a referendum on Trump. The media will be all over it."

Win or lose, Barletta has relished his experience with Trump and is proud that he was one of the first Republicans in Congress to endorse the president. "I would have been *the* first, but my staff kept talking me out of it. After I endorsed, I can't tell you how many people came up to tell me that I paved the way—I took the lid off. They said I gave them cover to say they were supporting Trump too.

"When I endorsed him, he had less than a one percent chance of winning. I was ridiculed. They were laughing at me. They're not laughing now!"

THE DEMOCRATS

SHOCKED BY THE Trump wave in 2016, Luzerne County Democrats and minorities are tiptoeing around still-triumphant Republicans and fellow Democrats who crossed over to vote for the president.

Amilcar Arroyo, the publisher of *El Mensajero,* a Hazleton-based monthly Latino newspaper that serves northeast Pennsylvania, describes an increasingly confident Hispanic population that now is the majority in Hazleton. But he also speaks warily of a man who since the election has been driving around the city in a black pickup truck that has an American flag on one side and a Confederate flag on the other. Arroyo takes this to be a Trump supporter's act of menacing defiance against the city's changing demographics.

Ben Medina, executive director of the Hazleton Integration Project, which works to smooth the entry of new Hispanic arrivals in Hazleton, says there is fear in the city. Fear that newly aggressive Immigration and Customs Enforcement agents under Trump may conduct raids at any time to deport people who are still waiting to become citizens.

Ron Felton, a former NAACP leader in Wilkes-Barre, says, "It feels different here under Trump now. You get the sense there's been an emboldenment among whites, not just in Luzerne but throughout Pennsylvania—a spiking of the football, a sense of, 'We're going to put you back in your place.'"

Alicia Mendoza Watkinson says that resentment toward immigrants and welfare recipients was the driving force behind Trump's support. Those feelings persist, and she still spends time dissecting the election, and debating the issues with friends who voted for the president. Since her father is Mexican American, it was difficult for Alicia—as well as for her older sister, Amanda Mendoza—to learn that so many people voted for Trump because of his pledge to build a wall on the country's southern border.

Johanna Habib Czarnecki, a committed Democrat who lives in prosperous (and Republican) Dallas, outside Wilkes-Barre, has lost friends over the election and continues to fight an anti-immigration mind-set among Trump voters, who, she says, remain convinced that Hispanics only come to the United States because they want to get on welfare and take advantage of the system.

Johanna's daughter, Alia Habib, has left Wilkes-Barre for New York and is glad she did. But she remains a keen observer of her hometown and is critical of what she thought was overly gauzy campaign press coverage that portrayed white working-class Trump voters in Luzerne County as the only ones who have endured hardships in the postindustrial Rust Belt. In this narrative, she says, Arab Americans like her and other minorities are cut out of the story entirely.

Amilcar Arroyo

Born in Peru, Amilcar Arroyo, who is sixty-nine, became a U.S. citizen in 1995. He arrived in the Hazleton area in 1989 to work on a farm, packing tomatoes. He then worked in a textile factory and a printing plant before launching *El Mensajero* in 2003. He has four people on his staff. Originally a Republican, Arroyo concluded that the GOP had drifted too far to the right in recent years, so he became a Democrat in

2012 to vote for President Obama, and he voted for Hillary Clinton in 2016.

Arroyo found Trump's election hard to accept. "Since the beginning, Trump was aggressive against the Mexicans. I'm not Mexican, but I'm an immigrant, and this made me feel bad," he says. "This is a country built by immigrants. Many Anglos don't remember that several generations ago, their ancestors came here from overseas too, like me, looking for a better life. So I didn't like Trump's anti-immigrant message, or the tone of his voice. I've lived here twenty-nine years now. To be president, you have to be impeccable, honest, and family-oriented. But this guy was opposed to those values. He's gone out with a porn star and a *Playboy* model while he's married. That's why I don't like Trump."

Arroyo feels that Trump won in Luzerne County on the coattails and legacy of Congressman Lou Barletta. "Trump won by such a large margin because it was a protest against immigrants in this area. That's why Trump won this county and why Lou Barletta is still so popular. He is still a congressman because Latino people don't go out and vote.

"When I moved here, there were only a handful of Latinos. All the troubles began when Lou Barletta passed that ordinance in 2006. But over the years since then, Latino immigration grew more and more—to the point where we are a majority in Hazleton now. So this city is a microcosm of what's going to happen in the U.S. in the near future: it will be a majority-minority country."

Arroyo believes Trump was elected because white people who did not vote in past elections came out to vote for him in droves. "We have to recognize that this guy who said Mexicans were rapists and criminals, and who spoke very badly about immigrants, is the president. I never heard that kind of talk from Obama, Bush, or Clinton. They were speaking in Spanish to get votes from Latinos! So Trump was the perfect guy for white, racist people: blond, blue eyes, with a lot of money."

Arroyo says the man in the black pickup truck is an outlier, not representative of most whites in Hazleton. "This guy drives through the city in defiance. His truck has an American flag on one side, in the back, and a Confederate flag on the other side. I don't know who he is. Looks like a young guy. He's alone. He doesn't yell anything. He's just making a statement—that he doesn't like us and we don't belong here. He's celebrating Trump."

To Arroyo, the Hazleton of today is a vibrant community with thriving Latino businesses. "This is not the Hazleton of 2006," he says. "It's rare to find an illegal here now. We're not afraid of Trump. I love this country and as an immigrant I will keep being a good citizen. I will keep paying my taxes. And I will see the immigrant community in Hazleton grow in good and positive ways. We have to suffer two years more. For Latinos, Trump has been a bad experience and we know we have to go out and make change in the next election. The blue wave is coming in the midterms and that's when the Republicans are going to pay for supporting Trump."

Ben Medina

But Ben Medina, of the Hazleton Integration Project, says Hispanics in the city do fear Trump.

"Legal residents here have members of their family who are not yet legal, and are in the process of getting paperwork, but it's very slow," says the forty-two-year-old Medina, who is Puerto Rican. "I know people who are waiting for papers to work, or to get their alien card, but the process is very long because of what Trump has been doing. So they're afraid. People live in fear in this town. We don't know what could happen. One day the federal agents could come to the city and make sweeps to pick up people. The fear is there."

Though Dominicans dominate the Hispanic population, Medina says that more and more Puerto Ricans are coming to the city. "We are helping them register to vote. After seeing how Trump humiliated the island after the hurricane, throwing paper towels around, they are getting registered."

Medina arrived in Hazleton ten years ago—three years after Lou Barletta, as mayor, made his headline-grabbing stand against illegal immigrants in the city.

"Barletta tried to close the door on Hispanics. He said he didn't want illegals, but it wasn't just illegals: it was Hispanics generally. Still, people have come anyway. I didn't know why, given what Barletta said and did. I would ask them that. They said they just saw an opportunity. There were jobs here. It's affordable, and a good place to raise kids."

Like Arroyo, Medina thinks Trump capitalized on the anti-immigrant tone established by Barletta in Luzerne County. "I think a lot of people voted for him because of all his statements about sending Mexicans back. The immigration issue was very important."

He believes Trump has damaged the United States in his presidency to date. "I've seen many changes under Trump. Our image abroad is bad and people have bad opinions about us. So I don't think he's making America great at all. Actually, Trump has divided the country—especially whites and Hispanics. A lot of Hispanics think whites are against us. But I don't think that's true. There are a lot of good white people. Still, a lot of people are divided, and that's not making America great again."

Whites, Medina says, should look at history and share the wealth. "Let's go back to the Indian people. They were here before the white people came and took over. So why would whites not be comfortable, when their ancestors came to this country as immigrants too? Now they can't accept others? Is this land given to them? I don't think so."

Ron Felton

Ron Felton, sixty-five, is from New Jersey and moved to Wilkes-Barre in 1989 after being transferred there by his employer, Prudential insurance.

"Some of us were concerned about moving to this area," he recalls. "I was told this area was twenty years behind the civil rights movement, so some African Americans had come down to talk with us in New Jersey. When we first moved here, Wilkes-Barre was about ninety-seven percent white. Today it's twenty-five percent minority."

Felton got involved in city affairs and eventually became president of the local NAACP and served in that position for eighteen years. He was outspoken and held a series of "diversity picnics and racial summits" to help bring about social change locally.

"The agenda was to promote racial harmony," he says. "It was an atmosphere where people could come with their preconceived biases in terms of stereotypes. I feel diversity is good because when we respect one another, we get along. I think everyone should have pride in who they are, but your pride should not come at the expense of someone else's."

Felton was running the NAACP meeting in Wilkes-Barre in 2008 that had been called to protest the rise of hate groups in the area when Steve Smith of Keystone United arrived with about twenty-five of his followers and asked to speak.

"I remember him coming with quite a few people," Felton says. "Not just guys. He brought some women. I said no, we weren't going to provide them with a platform to promote their hate. They almost outnumbered us. A lot of my people were becoming afraid."

Felton says he was not surprised that Trump won Luzerne County and Pennsylvania. "I thought he'd win in this area. Pennsylvania ranked fourth or fifth in the country in hate groups, and Luzerne County and northeast Pennsylvania have a lot of Klan and skinhead groups. However, with this county being mostly Democrat, I knew a lot of people would have to cross over to vote for Trump, and that's what happened. I feel that Trump's whole campaign was based on dividing the country, basically. He won by dividing, and by suppressing the minority vote.

"When Obama campaigned the first time, a white supremacist said he hoped he'd win because he felt it would
increase their recruitment efforts, and I think it did. There
was this talk when Obama won that we were in a post-racial
era. I never believed that. There's a lot of work still to be
done. The country was already divided and what Trump did
was exploit those divisions. Today I'm experiencing a similar
atmosphere that my father-in-law used to tell me he experienced. I was hoping that my son and grandchildren would not
have to experience the atmosphere that exists in this country
today—like 'Make America Great Again.' That's code. When
was America *not* great? Are you talking about going back to
the fifties, when blacks were subservient and were being degraded? Is that what you're talking about?"

Alicia Mendoza Watkinson   *Amanda Mendoza*

Alicia Mendoza Watkinson, thirty-five, works in customer
service for an electric company in Scranton. She grew up
in crime-ridden South Wilkes-Barre and now lives with her
husband in Hanover Township, a middle-class suburb. Life

is less stressful there than in South Wilkes-Barre, a drug-infested community where Watkinson says the murder rate is higher per capita than in New York or Philadelphia. Her parents and older sister, Amanda Mendoza, still live in South Wilkes-Barre—which is about one-third white, one-third black, and one-third Hispanic—and Watkinson worries about their safety.

"There was a shooting two doors down from my sister recently," Watkinson says. "Nineteen shell casings were found. It was a drug house. People pull out syringes in front of my parents' house and shoot up. They literally can't make it down the street without seeing drug dealers. If it was up to my mother, they'd be gone, but my father won't move. The mortgage is paid off and he's retired. He just shuts the windows. He has the mentality, 'I'm not gonna let these people drive me out of my neighborhood.'"

Amanda Mendoza says there were actually twenty-one shell casings found after the shooting. "We were petrified," she recalls. "I think it's the Bloods that are there, dealing heroin. We complain to the police, but they don't do anything. They just say, 'Don't approach these people, get their plate numbers.'

"This area is changing so much demographically, and that had a lot to do with why Trump did well here. We're getting a lot of inner-city kids from New Jersey and New York flooding this area because of cheap Section 8 housing. The whites feel increasingly uncomfortable here. I'm looking to get out but I'd have to take a loss on my house."

Mendoza, forty, teaches AP history at Meyers High School, which she attended in her youth. During the campaign, she says, a lot of what Trump said scared her, but she was not surprised he won because many of her own friends voted for him.

"There was a lot of misinformation out there," Mendoza says. "They believed what he said and he won. They said he was an outsider and making valid points. But when I showed them facts to prove that a lot of what he was saying was wrong, they didn't want to hear it. They just liked him. The thing that hurt me is a lot of people supported Trump because of building the wall, and I'm Mexican by descent. It caused some problems. My Mexican American father was born and raised here. He married an Irish lady."

Whereas some in Wilkes-Barre and other parts of Luzerne County tend to look askance at natives who move away, Watkinson says that's not her view.

"If you can get out of here, I congratulate you. We call ourselves lifers when we're stuck here. I'm sure you know how depressing this place is. Oh, absolutely. I live here, and it's not what it was. You don't want to walk around at night now. A lot of people took that fear and said, 'Trump is going to do something.' People attribute the crime to Hispanics or people who are not from here.

"This is a very racist area. It's bad. It really is. The area is not what it was, and a lot of people say it's because of the Hispanics, or African Americans. But as far as drugs are concerned, in the end, it's supply and demand, and the white males have the demand. We have a huge opioid problem here, yet people don't want to blame their own kids. They want to blame the Hispanic drug dealers. We're also a big welfare area, and that's another thing people looked at in the election."

Watkinson says Trump capitalized on this social upheaval

by running a fearmongering campaign. "I would say immigration was the main thing—saying he was going to have all these people deported, not just Hispanics, but Middle Eastern people."

Yet she has friends who voted for the president, and she is still trying to sort out what happened with them.

"My friend for twenty-seven years was gung ho with Trump. The arguments were more, 'Why do you hate Hillary so much?' I'd get answers like, 'She let her husband cheat on her. If she can't control him, how will she control the nation?' Then I'd bring the Russia investigation to their attention. The reaction? 'Well, we needed a change.' I said, 'You're getting change. Democracy is crumbling.' If they said Benghazi or the emails investigation were their reasons, I'd say, 'That's great, but what policy does Trump have that you agree with?' They really couldn't answer that. They just liked him.

"Trump still has his base here. Sometimes I think it's the stubbornness of not wanting to admit they voted for him. But they hated Hillary. There was such disdain for her. At his rallies, what people were wearing was appalling. And what they had their children wearing. Still, to this day, I see bumper stickers, like 'Hillary for Prison.'"

When Trump was elected, Watkinson was devastated.

"I'll say it—I cried. In this area, being liberal, as I am, is very frowned upon. I defend myself a lot, though sometimes I just keep it zipped to avoid conflict. The Trump people say, 'Give him a chance,' or 'Get over it. Deal with it.' But that's not me. I'm not going to get over it. I'm gonna fight as hard as hell to change things."

Johanna Habib Czarnecki

Johanna Habib Czarnecki, seventy-three, is an activist Democrat who volunteered tirelessly for President Obama during his first run for president in 2008, even putting up Obama campaign workers in her house. Today, she feels badly that she didn't work as hard for Hillary Clinton in 2016.

"I worked much harder for Obama, because this area is so prejudiced," says Czarnecki, who lives in Dallas, the well-to-do and heavily Republican suburb of Wilkes-Barre. "I did not think a person of color would fly here. People here are very color conscious and proud of their ethnicity, and don't like to let other people in—especially people of color. This is one of the reasons Trump won here: because they don't want to accept people of color. They don't like Mexicans, or the Hispanic population that has developed here and in Hazleton."

Though she is white, Czarnecki, whose father and grandfathers were coal miners, says she's felt the sting of being rejected too. "In high school, I took a test for Bell Telephone. This was in the sixties. I was told my last name was too long and had too many syllables. They wanted Smiths and O'Haras. That was the attitude. My maiden name was Siscavage. That's Lithuanian. White ethnics were not good enough. Too many vowels, I was later told. Their excuse was, it was easier for customers to say 'Miss Smith' than 'Miss Siscavage.' Today you can't be as explicit, but these attitudes persist. In my neighborhood now, if a person of color moved in, the neighbors would have a heart attack. In Dallas, they definitely don't want people who are not like them."

Czarnecki also witnessed firsthand the discrimination that her first husband, who was Syrian American, faced in Wilkes-Barre. Michael Habib owned a bar, and in the aftermath of the 9/11 attacks in 2001, his customers started telling him to his face where the United States should bomb those "sand niggers" back to. Habib's parents had been born in Syria, but he was American-born, he was Christian—not Muslim—and he was always the first person on his block to put a yellow ribbon on his front door in support of U.S. troops. And their daughter, Alia, had to endure questions in school from classmates asking her why she had those "nigger lips."[1]

Michael Habib died of lung cancer in 2006. Johanna later married Joe Czarnecki, a retired math teacher and lifelong Republican who became a Democrat to vote for Obama in 2008. Joe has become active in the local anti-Trump resistance, to the great annoyance of his Dallas neighbors. He has a garage full of "Impeach Trump" signs, which he puts up periodically in prominent places around Luzerne County, only to see them quickly torn down.

As Trump steamrolled through the Republican primaries, Johanna made a strategic decision to temporarily change her party registration from Democrat to Republican so she could vote for Ohio governor John Kasich in the Pennsylvania primary in an effort to stop Trump. But Trump won the primary easily.

Still, Czarnecki wasn't that worried. She thought Hillary Clinton would win, and that Hillary would be well served by her local ties: her grandparents had lived in nearby Scranton and her father had been born there, plus one of her main surrogates, Vice President Joe Biden, was also born in Scranton.

"Hillary did not really appeal to me, but I assumed she would be a shoo-in," Czarnecki recalls. "I just showed up and voted. I think Hillary felt, 'Why campaign here? I'm going to take it anyway.' The Trump people were putting up all these signs, but to me they were such rednecks. I didn't think much of it. I thought the much more educated people would come out for Hillary, and all of this Trump business would blow over."

Czarnecki, who is pursuing a degree in business ethics at King's College in Wilkes-Barre, thinks Hillary also took the white working class for granted. "She's been a proponent of the white working class, and she thought they knew that. But she dropped the ball and did not remind the people of what she was all about. The working class, sometimes they just don't get it. They're frustrated."

Czarnecki says that Trump's appeal in Luzerne County was rooted in racism. "The people that I know that voted for Trump were either very racist or, I hate to say this, the losers.

Their failures were not because of the economy, and they were looking for a scapegoat for why they were not doing well. Trump gave them the excuse to say this.

"We actually lost two very good friends over Trump. They were a couple, and we were vacationing with them. We knew they were racist but had ignored it and laughed at it. But it reached the point where we just couldn't be with each other. Another one of my friends just wanted that wall up. That's all she cared about. She doesn't want anyone coming here from Mexico and freeloading. Getting on welfare and having babies. It's such a mind-set here. You can't convince people this is not happening."

Czarnecki was born and raised in Wilkes-Barre and her family has deep roots there. She lived in her great-grandfather's house for three generations.

"People who stay here mostly have family ties," she says. "Those who are bright leave."

That includes Czarnecki's daughter, Alia Habib, who, after graduating from high school in Wilkes-Barre, went on to Barnard College in New York, where she now lives and works as a literary agent.

Habib, forty, says the deep economic insecurity that came out of the collapse of coal and later the manufacturing industry in Luzerne County was a fundamental part of her upbringing as an Arab American raised in Wilkes-Barre. Yet in reading coverage of the 2016 presidential campaign, Habib thought there was an important ingredient missing: it was not only angry whites in the working class who were economically insecure; it was minorities and people like the Habib family. They were the forgotten people too.

Alia Habib

"In the wake of the election, there's been a steady stream of articles with headlines like 'The Places That Made Trump President' or 'The Humanity of Trump Voters' or 'Welcome to Trumplandia'—not to mention books like the best seller *Hillbilly Elegy*—that turn places like my hometown, which 'broke' Republican after voting Democrat for decades, into political fetish objects," Habib wrote in an article for Buzz-Feed in January 2017. "After years of obscurity, the Rust Belt I grew up in is suddenly at the center of conversations about the 'white working class,' their crucial role in Trump's victory, and their future under his presidency . . . I've watched this phenomenon with increasing dismay as, over and over, the economic and cultural 'crisis' in the small, postindustrial cities and towns that dot the Northeast and Midwest is presented as some exquisite torture felt only by *white* Americans. In this narrative, people of color—people like me—are white-washed out of the story entirely."

And thus made to feel even more politically and economically marginalized. This is what President Obama referred to as the "zero-sum game" of American prosperity in his farewell address to the nation before he left office. "If every economic issue is framed as a struggle between a hardworking white middle class and undeserving minorities, then workers of all shades will be left fighting for scraps," he said.

For Habib, the story is not homogeneous. And the elegiac nostalgia that Trump's "Make America Great Again" slogan conjured up was a phony siren call.

"I think there's a lot of self-delusion about imagining that the sixties and seventies in Luzerne County were some kind of utopia," she says. "The nostalgia has more to do with seeing that people are different around them today."

She says she occasionally faced explicit racism growing up, like being called a "sand nigger" or a "camel jockey."

"My dad would hear 'sand nigger' directed toward him, and I had it used against me a few times. You'd hear about it after any flare-up in the Middle East. The first time I heard it, I asked my mom, 'What's a sand nigger?' And the same when I was called a camel jockey. Once my mom went to a neighbor's house and said, 'You can't call my daughter a camel jockey.' My mother would always fight back."

But more often, the racism was implicit. "People constantly asked me, 'What are you? What race are you? Are you white?' It was constant. I thought, *I must look really strange if people keep asking me this*. And I wasn't sure. I'd ask my mom, 'Are we white, or what?' I'd look up Syria on the map. What I wanted more than anything was for people to say, 'Okay, you're white. You're in.'"

But Habib was never allowed in. She loved to read and excelled academically, yet she felt "a deeply anti-intellectual vibe," and that it was never cool to do well in school. She never thought she was someone who could be dated or thought of as attractive. She actually made up a fake name—Lauren—in an attempt to be more accepted, but never used it. "My friend said, 'Alia, no one is going to start calling you Lauren!'"

Off at Barnard, Habib felt liberated. "I was surprised that people think I'm pretty! It was shocking to me. Or that people like that I'm smart. I never looked back."

She thinks many whites in Luzerne County view issues such as drugs, welfare, and crime through a racial prism.

"There is this sense among a lot of people that blacks and Latinos are getting more benefits than they are—to the town and county's detriment. This is a very widely held view. A sense that 'they are taking from people like us'—taking jobs and safety in the community—and that's consciously or unconsciously part of what Trump spoke to. And Wilkes-Barre has a crime problem that is understood in racial terms. Newcomers are seen as drug dealers or benefit scammers. I think this informed people's vote, and there was no sense that the Democrats helped *them*—just people of color.

"I am not linking Luzerne County's socioeconomic problems to its immigrants and people of color—quite the contrary. I do think that many Trump voters made that erroneous link, one that the candidate absolutely exploited and encouraged. Our country has a shrinking middle class, and stable and well-paid working-class jobs are even more elusive. People of color and immigrants suffer even more from these trends than anyone else; that's as true in northeast Pennsylvania as it is anywhere else. I don't think the next four years will see the residents of Luzerne County better off, but I do think it will become even harder to live there—economically, socially, emotionally—if you number among one of the groups Trump scapegoated. That's what breaks my heart."

EPILOGUE

With only some reservations, the men and women of Luzerne County that I interviewed for *The Forgotten* give Donald Trump high marks after eighteen months of his presidency, and all but one say if the 2020 election were to be held now, they would vote for the president again.

They point to Trump's two main legislative achievements—getting conservative Neil Gorsuch confirmed to the Supreme Court and pushing through a major tax cut—while presiding over a strong economy and bringing North Korea to the negotiating table. They also cite Trump's record of keeping campaign promises like streamlining government regulations, routing ISIS, curtailing legal and illegal immigration, improving services for veterans, revamping the country's position on trade deals, and recognizing Jerusalem as the capital of Israel.

On the negative side, most wish Trump would curb his relentless tweeting, and they fault him for not delivering on promises to replace Obamacare and get an infrastructure bill passed. They fully agree with Trump that the Russia investigation is a baseless witch hunt, and they defend the constant chaos and personnel churn at the White House as the necessary by-products of a change agent trying to "drain the swamp" in Washington.

LYNETTE

Despite the family angst the election has caused her, Lynette Villano remains a preening Trump peacock.

She wakes up excited and eager to embrace each day of the tumultuous Trump presidency. Without fail, she wears her Trump pin for all to see when she goes out in public. She recently bought a new white Ford Escape Titanium, and to make her political allegiance clear, she affixed to it two magnets—one on the driver's door and one on the passenger door—that read "TRUMP" in all caps. "Yes, he is my president."

As she drives, typically listening to fifties rock on satellite radio, the music will occasionally be interrupted by a pinging sound on her dashboard console letting her know that a new Trump tweet has arrived.

"I still continue to be approached daily with positive reactions to my Trump pin or my car magnets," she says. "It's just like before the election—people are so anxious to share their support for our president."

For all the ups and downs of the daily news cycle in the Trump era, Lynette plainly relishes the excitement of being part of the political fray. She is ready for anything that might happen—like the time she was attending a local political fund-raiser and was seated with a handful of people she didn't know. During small talk, when asked how she was doing, Lynette gave her stock, rather dramatic reply: "I wake up every morning and say to myself, 'Donald Trump is our president, so my day doesn't get any better.'"

In her circle, people will normally smile, agree with her, and start talking about how unfair the media is to Trump. But in this instance, there was silence. Nonetheless, Lynette forged ahead. She said that whenever people say anything negative about Trump, she politely reminds them that it's better than having Hillary in office.

At that, one of the women at the table stood up and told her husband she would wait for him in the car. She then proceeded to tell Lynette that she was actually one of Hillary's biggest supporters and couldn't stand Trump. Then she walked out.

Her husband turned to Lynette and said with a smile, "Don't pay attention to her. She's from Massachusetts!"

"I thought the whole thing was humorous," Lynette recalls. "She deprived herself of enjoying an event because she cannot tolerate sitting with a Trump supporter. Sad!"

But she despairs over the extent of hostility to Trump, how divided the country remains, and how entrenched she believes media bias against the president is.

"The hatred expressed by the media and other groups is overwhelming. I can't believe how vicious the attacks have gotten. I think I need to go off Facebook for a while. People are nuts! Never in my wildest dreams did I ever think it would be this bad."

Media bias, Lynette believes, is a key factor driving the country's divisiveness.

"There are certain media outlets that, no matter what he does, they will never cover Trump fairly, and there is nothing he can do to unite them. It's amazing how the same event is looked at so totally different! I do try and watch various news stations, and it is unbelievable, the difference in reporting. I have listened to the most vile, sick, degrading, and ugly things said about our president and his family on a daily basis."

Trump's regular press bashing on Twitter is its own provocation, of course, but Lynette casts this as the president skillfully playing defense and baiting his opponents to overreact. "He is a master at getting the media hysterical," she says admiringly. "I think he knows exactly what he is doing. His base loves it and it drives all the others wild.

"I don't think he is losing support, and if anything, the perception is the media are out to get him. Things such as jobs, taxes, health care, the wall, Second Amendment, and 'Drain the swamp' are the things I hear from people."

Lynette pronounces herself more than satisfied with Trump's performance in office to date. "People are really happy and feel America's strong again, that we have a leader who's going to stick up for America, not apologize for America. They don't know what Trump will do. That's strength. And he's finally letting the military run things."

Lynette is dismissive of what Trump's critics see as significant and discordant blemishes on his presidency, such as the Russia investigation, how he handled the neo-Nazi march in Charlottesville, and his attacks against National Football League players for kneeling during the national anthem.

"Week after week there still does not appear to be any

evidence of Trump-Russia collusion or proof that any votes were changed," Lynette complains. "Wasn't that the reason for the Mueller investigation from day one? There was no reason to collude with anyone. Trump won because of his message and people being tired of the 'swamp' in Washington. The people that hate Trump are exuberant about the Russia investigation, and all the Trump supporters just accept it as the rantings of the Left."

On Charlottesville, Lynette agrees with Trump that both the white supremacists and those who opposed them were equally responsible for the violence that ensued.

"The white supremacist group is such a small percent of our population. It's a shame they get so much attention. In America today, it is unreal that we have so much hate and violence—yes, on both sides. I say both sides because of all I have encountered myself since the election—like being called a Nazi because I support our president. Obama was elected by the voters and I'm sure many of them were white. People disagreed with his policies, not his color. But if you disagreed at all, you were labeled a racist. How are we ever going to change the future if we are constantly trying to change the past?"

As for the NFL players, Lynette says that Trump had a perfect right to express his view that what they were doing was wrong and disrespectful to the flag. And she says the players forgot that spectators and television viewers want to watch good football, not political protests.

"Since I don't follow, watch, or attend any sports events, I can only sympathize with my many friends who have expressed their frustration of politics being brought onto the field. They just want to watch a game. I also don't get the 'It's their First Amendment right' argument. No one is stopping their First Amendment right. But don't others have a right to disagree with their actions? Men and women volunteer to serve our great country every day, and if the president expresses his outrage at the disrespect that is exhibited, I guess that is *his* First Amendment right."

DONNA

After the election, Donna Kowalczyk took tentative steps to mend fences on social media. She friended the people on Facebook she'd previously unfriended, blaming the disconnect on some technical Facebook glitch.

She's posting about Trump again but still getting negative replies, so she says she may start posting under a pseudonym. When she sees "ridiculous anti-Trump posts, I try to be the adult and say, 'Come on, let it go. We don't need this nonsense.' "

She finds that her personal relationships are still frayed, and she's frustrated that she can't celebrate Trump's win more openly in predominantly Democratic Wilkes-Barre.

"I can't believe people are now saying about Trump, 'He's not my president!' " Donna says. "People are attacking people. Families don't speak to each other anymore. My neighbor who hates Trump with a passion—we don't talk about it. That's what you do. You just don't talk about it. I wonder where I'll go now. The Republican Party is small and nonexistent in this area. How we even got a Republican on the

Wilkes-Barre city council is amazing. I'm still reveling in Trump's win, but I can't celebrate here."

She's proud of her vote and thinks the president is doing a bang-up job, despite intense opposition from Congress, a hostile media, and a still-divided electorate.

"I think he's trying so hard, and I actually think he's getting more supporters, but people are still staying undercover, because they're afraid they'll be ridiculed or threatened," Donna says. "There's no more compassion. Why is that? I think a lot of people are jealous of him—your everyday person and politicians too—because he's been so successful in his life."

She dismisses the Special Counsel's investigation into ties between Russia and the Trump campaign, along with the related congressional investigations, as a "joke. I don't think there's anything to it. If they find something, they will have made it up. In Wilkes-Barre, they make things up politically all the time. And whatever the Russians may have leaked on Hillary was the truth, so what does it matter? People had their minds made up anyway."

Donna likes that Trump has occasionally reached out to Democratic leaders in Congress to try and do business, though little or nothing has come of it. "Trump's a reasonable person and just trying to find solutions. He's not a true Republican, so the other Republicans are seeing this move as a threat."

Though the campaign has long been over, Trump has reveled in keeping its spirit alive by staging "victory rallies" in certain parts of the country, and Donna has attended two of them in Pennsylvania.

The first was in Hershey on December 15, 2016, just

before Trump took office, while the second, in Harrisburg, celebrated his first hundred days in the White House. Donna says the Harrisburg event felt like a family reunion of sorts.

"It was so cool. Vice President Pence, Kellyanne, and the whole gang were there. No matter what anyone says, if you listen to Trump talk, you think you can conquer the world. He inspires you.

"It was so nice to be around like-minded people. I'll never go back to being a Democrat. Those people are crazy! I listen to Fox News now, and I never had before. The liberals think they'll get Trump out of office, but they never think about what would come next. They'd get Mike Pence, and he's more conservative than Trump!"

KIM

Critiquing Trump's first year in office, Kim Woodrosky especially liked the president's bombing of Syria: "I think we looked like a wet dishcloth for years. It was certainly time to stand up. After all, we're supposed to be the greatest country in the world."

She wishes Trump could get rid of sanctuary cities: "I think that's bullshit. I think the courts are making things so hard for him that nothing might get done."

On health care, Kim says the Republicans and Trump should have had their own plan ready to go when he took office. "The Republicans have been dying to get rid of Obamacare for so long and they don't even have a plan? If you'd been bitching about a problem your whole life, wouldn't you have a solution? All the country has wondered all these years was why we couldn't be bipartisan and get things done. And here we have a Republican president and a Republican Congress and still nothing gets fucking done? Come on!"

Kim thinks most voters would not support a tax increase to solve the seemingly intractable health-care issue because conservatives would demonize it as "socialized medicine," but she now says she might be ready to adopt a solution Republicans have long resisted. "I'm ready to support single payer. It's come to that, I think."

The Russia investigation? "I think it's all bullshit. They're just beating a dead horse. I'm convinced that Russia did not want Hillary Clinton as president, but whether there was this big collaboration with Trump and his people to make it happen is another question."

As for Trump's alleged affair with the porn star Stormy Daniels, Kim says, "No one cares. When we elected Trump, we knew he wasn't a choirboy. Do I believe her allegations? Certainly possible! But people can see right through her. She wants the publicity. Sometimes any publicity is good publicity, but her fifteen minutes of fame are over with the public."

Kim agrees with Trump that the media are out to get him. "The president can't get a break. When the media reaches for a story about his wife's shoes, I mean, come on. Of course they're biased against him. I've never seen a president get so much bad fuckin' press!

"Still, the first eighteen months of Trump's presidency have been nothing but remarkable. The economy is up, the unemployment rate is at an all-time low, he is making changes in the NAFTA agreement, the illegal immigration has slowed down, and we are in talks with North Korea. He has hit many of the points he promised pre-election. On a scale of one to ten, I would give him a solid eight . . . Trump for 2020!"

TIFFANY

Tiffany Cloud likes the Neil Gorsuch Supreme Court appointment and the muscle flexing of the Syria bombings. "Being humble is good, but there's a difference between being humble and apologizing, the way Obama did.

"I give Trump high ratings on deregulation, getting out of deals that were not good for us, and improving trade," Tiffany says. "I think the tax plan is a move in the right direction. I think the VA needs further improvement. I respect the strength he's shown to North Korea, though I wish he wouldn't use the language he has when talking about the leader there, who I find fundamentally unstable. But I agree with [Trump's] showing strength again on the world stage."

On the negative side, Tiffany says, Trump needs to better adapt his brash private sector style to the public sector. She says he is learning that "things in Washington don't work like corporate America." She counsels less tweeting and more patience.

"Trump is the businessman who's used to being first to market. Politics is not always about being first to market. Sometimes there's something to be said for a bit of patience."

Tiffany notes that the administration's health-care and travel restriction rollouts were botched, and she believes Trump should have tackled infrastructure first in hopes of getting Democratic and union support.

"Had he done that, perhaps the schism in the country might have narrowed," Tiffany says. "I wonder sometimes, though, if there's anything he can do that the Left would applaud or acknowledge. I don't know, but I think people should wish success for our nation. I remember watching Obama speak, and wishing him success after his inauguration. But Trump has been wished nothing but failure from the Left, over and over again."

Longer term, Tiffany believes that Trump will have to deal with health care rather than keep delaying a day of reckoning. "He touted himself as a great negotiator, a man of action, someone who can get the legislature to act, yet this area, thus far, is one where the action has yet to garner the results many Republicans want, so it's an area many will continue to watch closely."

Tiffany thought the firing of FBI director James Comey was appropriate and deserved. And while she tolerated the appointment of Special Counsel Robert Mueller to investigate the Russia affair, she thinks he should have had a broader mandate to look into Hillary Clinton's lapses as well.

"If a Special Counsel being appointed, and all the taxpayer money his investigation will cost, are what is needed to move forward to get media discussion and political activity focused on issues like jobs, health care, national security, et cetera, so be it," she says. "As a broad point, I just wish the Left and many in the mainstream media had been as enthusiastic about a special investigator looking into Clinton's activity, ranging from possible lies and cover-ups about

Benghazi to the accepting of funds from foreign nations into the Clinton Foundation and seeing if a quid pro quo existed, as well as the mishandling of classified emails, and the Loretta Lynch–Bill Clinton meeting during an active investigation of Hillary."

Tiffany believes that the good things Trump has done as president far outweigh the controversial statements he's made. As for Trump's handling of the white supremacists' march on Charlottesville, Tiffany launches into a careful defense in which she says substance will ultimately prevail over mere rhetoric.

"As I speak with Trump's most ardent supporters and even those who voted for him with lukewarm enthusiasm, their focus is less on his exact words," she says. "It's more on his definitive actions, such as a conservative on the Supreme Court, moves on illegal immigration, crackdowns on gangs and drug trafficking, choice for veterans in medical care, restructuring trade deals, deregulation, advances in the destruction of ISIS, and the rebuilding of our military.

"Now, make no mistake: what happened to people in Charlottesville was deplorable, just as what happened in Dallas when police were picked off at a Black Lives Matter rally was also deplorable. Hate, particularly when it results in violence and death, is an awful thing. And the president could have articulated a message following the Virginia events much better. But will Trump's word choice, on the heels of Charlottesville, erase everything else that people are seeing as good progress? As much as the Left might hope so, it's unlikely."

Overall, assessing Trump's time in office thus far, Tiffany

gives him an eight and a half out of ten. "You have to be constantly earning my vote every day. And so far, he has my vote again."

VITO

Vito DeLuca is more critical of Trump than the others. It is a measured criticism, much of it based on policy differences he knew he already had with the president, as well as Trump's brash style, which he also certainly knew about.

"I think the economic climate is better off than it was a year ago, but we're worse off in some respects too, like the environment," Vito says. "And I'm concerned with how his rhetoric is affecting race relations. I think a side effect of his in-your-face style is that he says many things that can be misconstrued or misinterpreted."

He reserves judgment on how beneficial the tax cut passed in late 2017 will be to him personally and to the country, but he thinks Trump is proving to be an able steward of the economy. "I think he's a guy who wants to put America first, and bring back offshore money. Toyota and others have announced plans to build plants in the U.S. I think he's doing what he can to help companies prosper."

Vito views the Russia investigation as mostly an attempt by Trump's opponents to undermine his presidency. "I'm really tired of both parties, when they lose, going after the other party criminally. If there's something there, I have to rely on law enforcement to make that determination. But until I see convictions for meaningful acts of treason, I'm skeptical. If there was conspiracy or some sort of collusion to affect our election, I certainly would have a problem with that."

Like many other supporters, Vito is disappointed by Trump's excessive use of Twitter, and the extent to which he is often baited into childish responses. "The president of the United States should be above responding to every jackass who takes a shot at him," Vito says, citing Trump's trivial feuds with the likes of comedian Kathy Griffin, LeBron James, and UCLA basketball father LaVar Ball. "Maybe that's part of his politically incorrect appeal, but no one else has ever done this. Anyone who'd been watching the evolution of how candidates reach the American voters knew that with the advent of Twitter and other social media, there was going to be a completely different dynamic. But Trump, instead of easing everyone into this concept, has taken it further, sooner, than I'm comfortable with. He's started talking almost in a stream of consciousness."

Trump's "I'm a genius" tweet was "like a sitcom," Vito adds, and the "Rocket Man" jabs at North Korean leader Kim Jong Un were "cringeworthy...I don't know if that gives the U.S. greater strength. I think Trump is Putin-like in some respects, as an authoritarian. But he also has that degree of recklessness where our foes might think, 'I don't know this guy won't kick my ass.' So, I don't know."

Vito admits to being disappointed by Trump's continued use of divisive tactics, though he does not blame him for the divisiveness in the country, since it existed long before the last election. "I do believe it is his responsibility to try and unite the country more, but the most important thing is to make sure that everyone can take part in the American dream, by starting a small business, or what have you. I don't know what is as important as making sure that the American dream is available to everybody. In other words, his record will count more than his rhetoric."

On the environment, Vito gives Trump bad marks, though he knew full well that Trump was no environmentalist when he voted for him, "so I got what I asked for. I'm not happy he discredits global warming, and most of his policies favoring the expansion of energy go against what I believe in. By expanding oil drilling and pulling out of the Paris accords on global warming, I think we're setting a bad example. On coal, the reason the regulations were in place was to limit emissions, and they were meant to protect the environment. For him to loosen those regulations and allow the coal industry to go forward seems to go against the environment... There is no coal industry here anymore anyway."

As for the continuing debate over whether Trump is presidential enough, Vito again says that voters knew what they were getting.

"We got what we asked for. But I would have liked to see him tone it down a bit after he got elected. He does not exercise even a nominal amount of discipline. He's very easily provoked. But people wanted something different, and that's what they got... I had hoped some of it was a shtick... Obviously, Trump's style of leadership is unorthodox—to be kind. It's mayhem unleashed at times, and it doesn't fit with any style of management I ever heard of. But what does it mean to be presidential? It means different things to different people in different eras, I am sure. In my opinion, in many respects President

Trump does not act in a way consistent with my image of how a president should act. That being said, I voted for him for the very reason that he did not act in a way consistent with my image of a typical presidential candidate."

Vito thinks Trump's critics should back off and let him do his job. "I did not vote for many of the presidents who served over the past thirty years, but when they were elected I treated them with the respect the office commands. I cannot believe the haters who are obsessed with bashing Trump on a daily basis. Some are people I have known for many years and consider friends. It is mind-blowing to me how they can expend the kind of energy they do to hate someone so intensely."

Meanwhile, Vito says he is still trying to get used to Trump's radically different approach to his job. "At this point, I have no idea who I am voting for in 2020. As far as I am concerned, Trump is auditioning for my vote right now."

ED

Ed Harry gives Trump an eight out of ten so far, citing the strong economy, the tax cut, and getting tough on trade. But he goes on to cite some specific disagreements, such as the president's choice of cabinet appointees. Some of those choices are contributing more to the swamp, rather than draining it, Ed believes.

Distressed by globalization, bad trade deals, and the loss of thousands of jobs to foreign countries, Ed was delighted that one of Trump's first acts as president was to withdraw from the Trans-Pacific Partnership.

"He also made the UN pay what they should," Ed says. "He took care of the VA, so now the vets can go to regular hospitals. GDP and the stock market are way up, a million new jobs, food stamps the lowest since the seventies. All that in spite of Congress doing nothing to help him."

With the tax bill now passed, Ed doubts the Democrats can take back the House in 2018. "If in fact ninety percent of people get tax cuts in their paycheck, then it will be tough to beat the Republicans. How will a congressman answer, 'Why didn't you give me a tax cut?'"

Labor should be with Trump, Ed believes, because he has moved to open offshore oil drilling, and if he can ever get his promised infrastructure legislation passed, that would create tens of thousands of new jobs that would further endear him to unions. Strategically, Trump erred in not tackling infrastructure as his first legislative priority, rather than health care, because he would have been more likely to win widespread Democratic support, Ed says, adding that the president often picks needless fights with Congress.

"One thing about Trump I don't understand is, I know he doesn't like John McCain and [Arizona senator Jeff] Flake and Bob Corker from Tennessee, but they have to vote for his legislation, so why pick on them? That's stupid."

Ed dislikes some of Trump's key appointments. "I don't like people from Wall Street and the swamp in the cabinet, but what experts are you going to get to run the economy unless you're in the game? If you're gonna deal with finance you need someone who understands it.

"Another disappointment I have with Trump is the people who he's appointed to the cabinet from the military: Jim

Mattis, H. R. McMaster, and John Kelly are all neocons. And Ivanka and Jared Kushner should be gone too. They have no business being in the White House, just because they're related to Trump. They're not qualified. They have no background on anything."

MARTY

On a scale of one to ten, Marty Beccone gives Trump a ten for his time in office so far.

"The economy, the tax reform bill, North Korea, the eradication of ISIS are all positive results . . . He got Gorsuch on to the Supreme Court, though the court was not a priority for me. The way the economy and jobs are going, along with my family and my safety—those are the most important things to me . . . I could do without the tweets."

Marty notes that Trump has kept campaign promises like streamlining government, eliminating at least the individual mandate component of Obamacare, curbing illegal immigration, and recognizing Jerusalem as the capital of Israel. "Bill Clinton, Obama, and George Bush all said they were going to recognize Jerusalem, but they didn't do it. Where the capital of Israel is doesn't affect me personally, but I like that Trump kept his promise."

Trump's slim record of legislative achievement—getting Gorsuch approved and the tax cuts—is not his fault but the Democrats' fault, Marty believes. "There's been no give-and-take from the other side. It's just 'the resistance.' Now it's strictly along party lines. There's no way a Democrat is going to remotely consider a Republican idea, and vice versa."

Is he concerned that Trump has had the lowest approval ratings of any president in modern times? "No, because again, ISIS is on the run, the stock market is at an all-time high, and my taxes are going down. I don't believe in any polls anyway. I guarantee you that if I took a poll, I could come back with a zero approval or a hundred, depending on how I asked the questions. Polls are bullshit. Write that down as a quote."

Marty agrees with Trump that the president *did,* in fact, win the election in a landslide. "Everybody describes it as a landslide. If you take away New York and California, those two states dictate the popular vote. If we had the popular vote decide the election, the Midwest would say, 'We don't want to be part of your country.' If you go by counties, the country is a sea of red, so it really *was* a landslide. The East Coast and West Coast cities are not this country. Without truck drivers and farmers, the people on the coasts would starve to death. Those people count just as much as the guy in California. That's why we have the electoral college."

Marty has closely followed the Special Counsel's investigation into possible collusion between Russia and the Trump campaign and is furious about it. Despite the fact that U.S. intelligence agencies have unanimously concluded that Russia interfered in the election by hacking into Democratic Party headquarters and the computer of Hillary Clinton's campaign chairman, John Podesta, Marty, like Trump, thinks the source is not necessarily Russia.

Nor has anyone confirmed to Marty's satisfaction that Russia disseminated the hacked material through WikiLeaks—

but even if it did, he thinks WikiLeaks performed a public service in doing so. Furthermore, he says, the Special Counsel's investigation has not established that there was collusion between Trump and Russia during the campaign, and the probe has been tainted by FBI bias against Trump.

Marty cites text messages exchanged by two FBI agents, Peter Strzok and Lisa Page, who worked on both the investigation into Hillary Clinton's email server and the Russia investigation into Trump. In the Clinton probe, when former FBI director James Comey wrote a preliminary report concluding that she had been "grossly negligent" in her handling of classified emails, Strzok reportedly suggested softening the conclusion to "extremely careless," a change that Comey ultimately adopted, thereby allowing the former secretary of state to escape criminal liability. Meanwhile, some of the texts about Trump, uncovered by the Justice Department's inspector general, were harshly critical of the then presidential candidate. The inspector general showed the texts to Special Counsel Robert Mueller, who then removed Strzok from his investigation into Trump. Page, a lawyer, had already left Mueller's team.

BRIAN

Brian Langan remains an enthusiastic supporter of the president and he has an array of Trump gear for himself and his family, including the popular "I Am a Deplorable" T-shirt, a reference to Hillary Clinton's infamous swipe about Trump voters; an "Adorable Deplorable" shirt for his daughter; a

"Don't be a Chump, Vote for Trump" shirt; and of course the classic "Make America Great Again."

But unlike many hard-core Trump supporters, Brian maintains friendships with a network of Democrats and Hillary supporters, and they disagree agreeably about politics. "If we disagree, I'll say, 'That's how you feel; this is how I feel,'" Brian says. "I don't want to lose any friends over politics. Who would?"

Looking at Trump's time in office thus far, Brian is pleased with the president's performance and thinks he is learning on the job: "He's getting some lessons. I didn't vote for him because he was a politician."

Brian is not bothered by Russia's intervention in the election because there is no evidence that Moscow tampered with the actual voting machines.

He says it's embarrassing that the Republicans still don't have their own health plan, after years of voting to repeal Obamacare. "If there's anything I can count on, it's the Republicans to shoot themselves in the foot. But I think they've gotten their feet under them a little better now, with the tax cut. There's always going to be the Never Trumpers on the Republican side, but more are working with him now."

On immigration, Brian favors doing a deal with the Democrats to give the so-called Dreamers a pathway to citizenship in return for some form of border security, which does not have to mean a wall stretching for miles and miles. "If we have border security, I don't care about a wall all the way. We can't have open borders, that's all."

Brian was delighted by Trump's two bombings of Syria.

Referring to the first, "He was saying, 'There's a new president now. You're getting fifty-nine tomahawks up your ass.'"

And he thinks Trump was right to fire FBI director James Comey. "Director Comey had put himself out in public positions these past two years, and I don't see that as his place. My law enforcement background says that an investigator should investigate, compile the facts, and present them to a prosecutor for a decision on prosecution or not. He was out there like he was an elected official. I find the Democratic reaction amusing, since many politicians on that side had been blaming Comey for interfering with and sabotaging Secretary Clinton's campaign. That issue and other issues where he had to correct the record after testifying in front of Congress a few times did make the public doubt the credibility of the FBI. The FBI issues were becoming too political, and that is dangerous for the future of the FBI."

Brian thought the appointment of Robert Mueller to investigate the Trump campaign's ties to Russia was unwarranted, and a case of overkill. "This situation is so overblown because it's President Trump. It's a twenty-four-hour-a-day, seven-day-a-week assault on him. I've been watching politics for a long time, and the things going on now are scary to me. I worry for our country."

He supports the president's prolonged, public shaming of his attorney general, Jeff Sessions, for having recused himself from the Russia investigation and for not doing enough to investigate Hillary Clinton.

"I think Attorney General Sessions is a good guy and a little under the gun, but this is a new era of a president who doesn't use the media for his messages like any other," Brian says. "His tweets are not always helpful, but in the big picture, I don't mind him tweeting. I can see the president's point that it's been some time now, and we haven't heard of any law enforcement agency looking into the DNC stuff, or the Clinton Foundation. I think maybe the president is trying to light a fire under the AG. I hope so, anyway. I'm optimistic that all this Russia investigation activity will prompt more of a look into the Clintons. I think the swamp is deep and strong, and it protects its own.

"I'll give the president an eight so far. No one is perfect. He is doing great considering he has the Democrats, establishment Republicans, the press, and Hollywood fighting him every step of the way. I shall vote for the president in 2020. I don't see any possible Democrat or Republican potential candidate coming forward that I would even consider."

THE VETERAN

Grading Trump after eighteen months in office, Erik Olson gives him an eight and a half out of ten.

"He's still a little crass, and do I wish he would not say some of the things he says? Yes. But there's nothing he could do to satisfy a portion of this country. He could walk on water and they would say he was contaminating the water. Yet I like to listen to others' views and not judge them, so I wish Trump would come across as more respectful of others.

"I think he's done a good job, but he is so different, and presents himself as so unpolished. I think people were just ready for such a dramatic shift in our nation's direction that he fit the bill. And the numbers turned off by Hillary helped his cause."

Erik thinks services for veterans have improved under Trump. "The VA is such a huge bureaucracy it's like trying to turn the *Titanic*. But I've seen some positive changes over the last year. Wait times have come down. They've come up with different ideas on how to handle claims for compensation, and I've found just getting medical appointments is easier."

On the Russia investigation, Erik sees no "there there. Were there any meetings? Maybe. Was there pure Putin–Trump collusion? No, and I think there's a huge witch hunt going on. If anything, with the dossier, the Russian investigation could go more in the other direction toward Hillary and the Democrats. I just think we should stop the endless investigations. That goes for both sides. And heal the great divide we have."

He faults Trump for failing on health care. "On health care, I'm pretty pissed off. I don't give anybody a pass on that. When it comes to health care, the Republicans railed against Obama for seven years! They had all those years to come up with a better plan, and when they had their chance, they didn't do anything. They dropped the ball."

Erik thinks transgender troops should be able to serve in the military. "Here's my take on that: transsexual or homosexual, if you're willing to ruck up, grab a rifle, and face the enemy with me, I don't care what you do. That's my view. I don't agree with what Trump did with that. I don't think it was the right subject to tackle then. If you're serving honorably, hey, keep on serving. I think most veterans feel the same way."

He gives Trump high marks on Iraq and Afghanistan. "I think we're doing fantastic, especially in Iraq. It's amazing what we've done there in the last year. ISIS was on the out-skirts of Baghdad. To see what the Iraq Army has done, with our support, is amazing. Iraq is free now. In Afghanistan, we don't know enough yet, but our shift in tactics is right. I al-ways said it should be more of a Special Forces fight. You can't kill your way to victory. You've got to try to rebuild a founda-tion for people to have a normal way of life. Too many drone strikes only creates collateral damage. You might kill one ter-rorist but create three others."

Erik is cautiously optimistic on North Korea. "That's an animal of a different color right there. There's no good an-swers. I think we've tried to placate them for the last twenty years and they're now more dangerous than ever. So, we're trying a different tactic and standing our ground. I don't like Trump's 'Little Rocket Man' stuff, but I think what he's doing is working. It's brought them to the negotiating table. I don't think that would have happened without Trump."

On immigration, Erik believes that the children born in the United States to illegal immigrants need to be reckoned with as part of a proper reform package. "Am I hard-core, boot 'em all out? No. Like with the Dreamers, there needs to be a path to citizenship for them. You can't just have an open bor-der, but you've got six or seven million here, and we need to get them out of the shadows and figure out what to do with them. The majority are decent members of society. Painting them all as freeloaders is unfair and I don't like that. So there needs to be proper immigration reform."

Erik is an avid hunter and an NRA member, but he dis-agrees with Trump's call to arm teachers following the mass shooting at a high school in Parkland, Florida, that killed seventeen people in February 2018. Putting police officers in schools would be more appropriate, he thinks.

"Though I belong to the NRA, I find myself more liberal on gun control than other guys. I'm a hunter and have rifles and shotguns, but I don't see the need to have high-capacity rifles with magazines, or semiautomatics. There's no reason an eighteen-year-old should get an AR15, but I'm not sure how raising the age will cure the problem, because if he wants to get a gun he'll get a gun. I'm not for gun control because that's a slippery slope. If you ban one kind of weapon, what comes next?"

THE WHITE NATIONALIST

Steve Smith participated in the national march for Trump in March 2017 and remains firmly in Trump's corner—largely because he believes the president has created a climate in which the white nationalist message can flourish. But he is critical of some of Trump's specific decisions.

One example is Trump's authorization of the Syrian missile strikes. "He said no foreign entanglements. We can't be the world's policeman. I don't want that."

Steve regrets that Trump fired Steve Bannon and dislikes the way the president has publicly criticized Attorney General Jeff Sessions. "The public shaming of Sessions was a bad move on Trump's part, especially since Sessions has been a supporter of Trump's since the beginning of his campaign."

Steve dislikes the choice of Nikki Haley as United Nations ambassador because she ordered the Confederate flag taken down when she was governor of South Carolina.

He agreed with the firing of FBI director James Comey but says it should have been done on Inauguration Day. "That whole situation became a distraction. Trump needs to concentrate on policies he promised to enact during his campaign, especially stopping illegal immigration, or he will be a one-term president."

Steve thinks the Mueller investigation is much ado about nothing, and he saw nothing wrong when Trump shared sensitive intelligence with top Russian officials during a meeting in the Oval Office. "Correct me if I am wrong, but the president can declassify information as he sees fit. The Cold War is over. Russia shouldn't be viewed as an enemy of the United States."

Steve says he is "in complete agreement" with Trump's ordering of a transgender military ban.

"Trump is far from perfect, but thus far he is the best president in my lifetime. Still, let's wait and see how he does. If he doesn't do what he promised, I'll vote for someone else in 2020, but as of right now, I intend to vote for Trump, though I don't put all my faith in him as a great savior. All politics is local, from the grass roots up. That's why I put my foot in the door here in local politics, and I'm going to take advantage of it.

"I'm just getting started," Steve promises.

THE CHRISTIAN

In January 2018, when news broke of Trump's involvement with the porn star Stormy Daniels in 2006, when he was newly married to Melania Trump, most evangelical leaders said they would give the president a pass on the issue. Astonished, Ray Harker was moved to violate the house rule against discussing Trump by writing his wife, Jessica, a letter, hoping that this development might shake her faith in the president. He shared the letter with me.

Jessica (My Luv),

...My faith hasn't been shaken, nor has my political ideology changed one iota over the last two years. But what has changed is that those same Christian leaders, whom I've looked up to and have been inspired by over the years, have no voice of authority anymore for me. Men like Franklin Graham, Tony Perkins, Robert Jeffress, Jerry Falwell Jr.... and most pastors in general. I have lost all respect. Bible-believing Christians can try and try to defend this evil man, their president, but there is no explanation that makes any biblical sense to me.

...This man (Teflon Don) has done one thing or another, over the last two years, on at least a weekly basis, that would (and should) have destroyed anyone else's political career... Trump sets a new precedent by which public figures from here on out will be judged. He has the luxury of a low moral standard. He has made a mockery of Republicanism and of our founders' divinely inspired election process. He has destroyed the dignity of the most sacred office in the land—more so than I could have ever imagined. He has set a new low standard of conduct and behavior by which our role models will now be held to. This isn't a man of God. Trump represents chaos, confusion, deception, dishonesty...impulsiveness, narcissism, general immorality, and he is nonideological (Trumpism). These are not only characteristics of Satan, but of every evil authoritarian who has ever lived. Look at Hitler, Mussolini...

Jessica was initially nonplussed about the Stormy Daniels issue.

"On and on it goes," she wrote to me in January 2018. "The one thing I would like to know is if anyone told that Stormy lady the good news of the Gospel. She needs Christ because she has defiled her body in so many ways. Evangelic Christians were not looking for a pastor when they voted for Trump. They were looking for someone who could beat Hillary Clinton and reboot America, because we were, and still are, in a tailspin."

But by March, Jess had a change of heart. She still felt Stormy had defiled her body and would have done better by seeking out Christ, rather than Trump. But she thought the president owed his wife and "the other women" he was alleged to have had extramarital sex with a public apology.

"I think he could then put this behind him, especially if he didn't know Christ at the time," Jess says. "I mean, how many men fall into porn because it is a trap from the pits of hell? That's what Satan does. He looks for a foothold, a weakness. Trump had money and could have whatever he wanted. It's sad he didn't honor his wife with exclusivity."

Despite the Stormy Daniels kerfuffle, Jess remains serene about Trump. These days she spends much of her time praying.

"The more I read the Bible, the more I'm in tune with the Lord and walking in his spirit," she says. "I love my nights. I go home and sit with the Lord. I read the Bible, but I don't just read it—I study it. If you look for God, he will be found. When you put God first, things just work. That's what my life is like. What fulfills me the most is being on fire for the

Lord. That means being honest, taking care of people, doing the most I can for our veterans, and being appropriate in how I come across to people. To act and dress like a lady. Not to use profanity, or be vulgar. Not to mock people."

Reminded that Trump mocks people regularly, Jess says, "It's because he's so frustrated. He's so upset with what people are saying that we're tapping into a psychotic side of Trump. Anyone can be pushed over the edge. I think he's like Mel Gibson in *Lethal Weapon*. He can be off in his mannerisms, with the way he responds to people, his tweets, how he's not humble."

But Jess notes that as president, Trump has been especially attentive to evangelicals, and he's delivered for them.

First and foremost, there was his Supreme Court appointment of the conservative Neil Gorsuch. Trump also rescinded President Obama's protections allowing transgender students to use preferred bathrooms in public schools. He signed a bill withholding federal funds from groups that perform abortions, including the Republican bête noire Planned Parenthood. He signed an executive order reinstating the so-called Mexico City policy, barring funds for international groups that perform or promote abortions. He signed an executive order promoting religious liberty, designed to give religious organizations greater freedom in political speech without having to pay an IRS penalty. He put evangelical Christians in prominent positions within his administration, such as Vice President Mike Pence, Secretary of Education Betsy DeVos, Secretary of Housing and Urban Development Ben Carson, and, as Secretary of Health and Human Services, Tom Price (though Price was later forced to resign following revelations that he used private charters and military planes for his travel). And Trump eliminated U.S. funding of the United Nations Population Fund, which critics have said supports abortions in China and other countries.[1]

Despite all that, Jess thinks Trump has "got a lot of room for growth...Sometimes his tweets make him sound stupid. People are waiting to see if he can stop that, or at least cut way back."

Jess says the media are hindering Trump's presidency. "They're not being fair and balanced. I know that's Fox News lingo, but the media generally are not reporting any of the good Trump is doing. And that's why people don't trust the press anymore. That's why 'fake news' has taken off.

"Saying Trump is not stable—do you know how much that's hurting the country? People have to get over their anger that Trump was elected. They have to start working with him rather than obstructing him, because it really is affecting America."

At this writing, in late June 2018, no one can be sure how the Trump story will end: with his indictment or even impeachment, if Robert Mueller's findings are grave enough, or with the president being triumphantly reelected in 2020.

No matter what happens, Trump thus far has surely left a mark like few presidents before him. He has constantly raised hell—tweeting and provoking, and almost totally dominating the news by ripping up the conventional presidential governing style and installing his own. He has fended off a spate of scandals and otherwise presided over a White House dominated by chaos and personnel turnover. Besides the Russia investigation, Trump is also facing six other significant legal cases: a sweeping lawsuit brought by the New York State attorney general accusing Trump's charitable foundation of violating campaign finance laws, self-dealing, and illegally coordinating with his presidential campaign; entanglement in the investigation federal prosecutors have launched in New York against Trump's longtime personal lawyer, Michael Cohen; a pair of lawsuits challenging his refusal to divest himself of his business interests while president, in violation of the Constitution's emoluments clause barring a president from accepting gifts or payments from foreign governments without congressional approval; and, finally, two separate defamation lawsuits from women he allegedly had sexual relationships with—the former porn star Stormy Daniels and Summer Zervos, a former contestant on *The Apprentice* who claims Trump sexually assaulted her in 2007. The president has denied the Daniels and Zervos charges, as well as the allegations raised in the other cases.

It has all been spellbinding but also exhausting to watch. One reelection variable for the president may be how much the electorate, even those who voted for him, will have suffered from Trump fatigue. A Pew Research Center report released in June 2018 found that a strong majority of Americans feel overwhelmed by the amount of news today: 61 percent of Democrats and 77 percent of Republicans.

Trump has rewritten all the rules, reminding Democrats still reeling from 2016 of the cliché that elections really do have consequences, and he has not hesitated to use his presidency as a political weapon. He's violated the supposedly sacrosanct boundaries separating the White House from the

Justice Department by relentlessly attacking the FBI and his own attorney general for either unfairly investigating him or for not investigating Hillary Clinton and his other enemies enough. Trump has also said he could pardon himself for any crimes resulting from the Special Counsel's Russia investigation, an investigation that he called "totally unconstitutional." And he has been consistently reluctant to condemn Russia for interfering in the 2016 election while continuing to issue charitable statements about Vladimir Putin and speaking regularly with him by phone.

Trump has even created an alternate reality. As of June 2018, the *Washington Post* reported that Trump had made 3,251 false or misleading claims as president, an average of 6.5 a day. That is astonishing enough, but Trump—with his regular press bashing and calling the media "enemies of the American people"—has been able to convince much of his base that the mainstream media are simply out to get him, that *they* are lying about *him,* and that therefore almost all of what they report is "fake news." And he has kept up a steady drumbeat that the Russia investigation is a hoax and nothing but a "witch hunt."

Long gone are the days when facts were accepted as facts. Now there is not even a consensus on what a fact is, and Kellyanne Conway, Trump's senior adviser and former campaign manager, has famously said that there are "alternative facts" to consider as well. Fox News and other conservative media have incubated the concept of two different realities: one pro-Trump, the other anti-Trump. And in 2016, the adjective "post-truth" was named word of the year by Oxford Dictionaries, whose editors described it as "relating to or denoting circumstances in which objective facts are less influential in shaping public opinion than appeals to emotion and personal belief."

Many of President Trump's ideas about the press are echoed by Luzerne voters. Trump is expert at creating a force field of perception around his base, and one way he does so is by questioning the manner in which he is perceived by the press. Whether or not the media have become more partisan under the current administration is an open-ended question; what is clear is that the president and his administration perceive this to be so, and they play on that message continually—especially in times of crisis.

Most people now only read or watch news that validates their own views. So there is Fox News, Breitbart News, and the Drudge Report for the Right, and MSNBC, CNN, and the *New York Times* and *Washington Post* for the Left. The Internet and Google have greatly diminished or eliminated the role of editors, as news consumers have chosen to become their own editors and seek out only the news they want, ignoring what they don't.

Substantively, wiping out the legacy of President Obama has been paramount to Trump. He's pulled out of the Iran deal, scrapped America's role as an honest broker for Middle East peace in favor of an open embrace of Israel, and exited the Paris climate agreement. He's dismantled Obama's multilateral approach abroad in order to install an America First agenda on foreign policy and trade, and he's strained the Atlantic alliance to the point of virtually telling Europe to go it alone. In early June 2018, Trump upended the G7 summit in Quebec City, first by saying Russia should be a member of the organization, and then by calling Canadian prime minister Justin Trudeau "very dishonest and weak" on trade, and refusing to sign a joint statement with allied nations that he had earlier agreed to. Such displays of pique toward America's traditional Western allies, just before the president went on to lavish praise on North Korean leader Kim Jong Un at the Singapore summit, provoked a fresh round of commentary that Trump has "dictator envy." That critique was bolstered when combined with the president's previous raves for Putin, for Chinese president Xi Jinping, and other strongmen like Philippines president Rodrigo Duterte or Egyptian president Abdel Fattah el-Sisi. To the extent there is a Trump Doctrine, one senior White House official described it to *The Atlantic's* Jeffrey Goldberg as "We're America, bitch."[2]

At home, Trump has appointed more than forty conservative judges, gotten a solid conservative confirmed on the Supreme Court in Neil Gorsuch, and won the chance to appoint another well-known conservative, Washington DC–based federal appeals court judge Brett M. Kavanaugh, to the high court after Justice Anthony Kennedy announced his retirement in late June 2018. The president has gutted and sabotaged Obamacare, albeit while failing to replace it with an alternative health plan. He's abandoned Obama's striving for a post-racial, integrationist agenda in favor of a retro-tribalism that is trending toward the old separate-but-equal ethos, as nearly sixty percent of Americans consider the president to be racist, according to a February 2018 poll by the Associated Press and the National Opinion Research Center (NORC).

Trump and the Republican Congress have enacted a tax cut for corporations and to largely benefit the rich, thereby ballooning the deficit and effectively eliminating a balanced budget as a traditional Republican priority. The president has eviscerated the Environmental Protection Agency, using administrator Scott Pruitt to pursue a carbon-first agenda, while opening up Alaska for oil drilling. (Pruitt was forced to resign in July 2018 in the face of a slew of ethics investigations that clouded his tenure.) And he has signaled that torture is back on the table for consideration with his appointment of Gina Haspel as the new CIA director.

More pragmatist than ideologue, Trump has totally rebranded the Republican Party in his own image by mixing populism with conservatism—a kind of conservatism that is unrecognizable to the traditional GOP and its now neutered Never Trump wing.

While many may see Trump as undisciplined, he has been laser-focused on delivering on key campaign promises, like curbing both illegal and legal immigration and dumping the free-trade orthodoxy that he thinks has been a bad deal for America.

"When he ended the TPP altogether, that was almost enough for me," Ed Harry says. "When he did that I was quite happy. That was the agenda for the labor movement for the last three years. Yet he got no credit for it. NAFTA? That's in the process of being renegotiated or ended. GATT the same thing." Now Trump is moving to slap tariffs on friend and foe alike, prompting fears of trade wars.

The president's support is mostly personal, not ideological. His core voters have stood by him through all manner of crises, including the June 2018 debacle at the Mexican border when Trump was forced to abandon his policy of separating immimigrant children from their parents, as well as the withering criticism he received the following month for fawning over Russian president Vladimir Putin at their summit meeting in Helsinki. Trump supporters remain intensely loyal to him—and he to them. Since winning the election, Trump has focused almost exclusively on maintaining the support of his base by creating an us-versus-them siege mentality, tending to his voters' emotional needs constantly on Twitter, continually bashing his enemies—especially the media—and holding regular rallies in favored states around the country to bathe in the applause of his followers, as if the campaign had never ended.

On its face, behaving more like the president of his base rather than the entire country would not appear to be a winning reelection strategy for Trump. But even some leading Democrats—such as Doug Sosnik, Bill Clinton's former political director—think that Trump, despite one recent poll[3] showing that 57 percent of all voters believe he is not fit for office, has a clear path to reelection.

"We have entered a new era in American politics," Sosnik wrote in the *Washington Post* last year. "The 2016 election exposed how economic, social, and cultural issues have splintered the country and increasingly divided voters by age, race, education, and geography. This isn't going to change. What have changed are the political fault lines that have driven the debate since the early 1980s. Until now, the ideological divides between the parties were largely differences around social issues, defense spending, and trade, as well as tax cuts for the wealthy and corporations. Today, the central issue has become populism as voters have moved away from the two political parties and increasingly self-identified as Independents."[4]

Since two of the last three presidents—Trump and George W. Bush in his 2000 campaign—were elected without winning the popular vote, securing an outright majority is now considered an increasingly unlikely goal, not a necessity.

Plus, declining voter support for both major political parties increases the likelihood that there might be a major third-party candidate who could further split the anti-Trump vote. Even the 2016 Libertarian and Green Party campaigns won nearly 5 percent of the vote between them—more than enough to tip the election one way or the other.

In an effort to reclaim their credibility with the working class, Democratic congressional leaders are ramping up their economic pitch with a plan called "A Better Deal," which seeks to increase government regulation of big business and to implement a sweeping infrastructure program that would be a boon for jobs.

But there are others who think the 2020 election will be won less on economics than on cultural issues like race and immigration, which voters in Luzerne County and elsewhere proved were pivotal in electing Trump.

"When Trump stands up in front of his audience at rallies during the campaign and tells them he's going to give them their country back, Trump is having a conversation about race," Cornell Belcher, a Democratic pollster who worked for Obama, told the *New York Times* in 2017. "Our response is that we are going to raise the minimum wage—we are having a conversation about economics. We are playing checkers while Trump is playing chess. And he continues to do so as he focuses on things like black NFL players taking a knee. Until Democrats can inoculate against some of the heightened angst, most prominently found among blue-collar whites, about the changing face of America, they will struggle to compete for white noncollege voters."[5]

Belcher argues that rather than concentrate on winning back the white working and middle class, Democrats would be better served by maintaining and expanding the Obama coalition of women, millennials, minorities, and the college-educated—especially as the United States edges ever closer to being a majority-minority country. This would essentially be doubling down on the hope that Trump's overwhelmingly white coalition cannot win mathematically, a hope that was shown to be wrong in 2016.

If culture bests economics, in order to make inroads in reclaiming the Trump vote, Democrats will need to develop more of a heartland sensibility and change the widely held perception that they are dominated by elites on either coast who look down on people in the middle of the country. In other words, they need to nominate someone more like Bill Clinton than Hillary Clinton, someone with the blue-collar cred that Hillary did not have.

Despite having pledged in his acceptance speech on election night to try and unify the country, Trump in office has attempted nothing of the sort, but his supporters don't seem to mind.

Lynette Villano concedes that Trump made the unifying pledge, but she now thinks he has too many enemies to follow through on it. "There is just as much responsibility from the Never Trump people, the Hollywood left, CNN, MSNBC, the *New York Times,* the swamp in DC, late-night TV, Black Lives Matter—I could go on and on," she says. "Half of the country hates the president. Do you really think there is anything he can say or do that will bring us together? I'm all for promoting civility, but we are so divided and people are so dug in, it's hard to have a conversation."

And Trump's hard line on immigration and the social strain it causes—levers to divide the country rather than unite it—remain popular with his base. Donna Kowalczyk takes the view that many in Luzerne County do: Their grandparents came to this country legally, so why can't the current generation do the same? "That message resonated in the campaign," Donna says. "Around here we have a lot of people from other countries who have insurance and can go to any doctor. They have Section 8, food stamps—they have it all. Whereas people who have worked their entire life can't get anything. That bothers me. I don't know where people got this whole 'racist' thing about Trump. Yes, he wants to get rid of illegals. But he's right. We should take care of our own first."

Despite delivering for his supporters in the culture wars, Trump's policies as president have not always been in his supporters' economic interests.

While he has presided over a strengthening of the already strong economy he inherited from Obama, Trump has not followed through on many of the economic metrics he touted in the campaign. For example, he promised to eliminate the national debt in eight years, but the budget he filed in February 2018 anticipates adding $7 trillion to the debt over the next decade. While he campaigned on the high costs of the wars in Iraq and Afghanistan and said the money could be better used at home, his budget increased defense spending by $195 billion. And while he promised to level-fund or increase spending for key entitlements like Medicare and Medicaid, his budget cut $554 billion in Medicare spending over the next decade, $250 billion from Medicaid, and $214 billion from food stamps. His promise to enact a $1 trillion infrastructure program, which could create tens of thousands of new jobs, is stalled and seems to be going nowhere, while his tax cut bill overwhelmingly benefits corporations and the rich, not the working and middle classes.[6]

But Trump's base continues to love him anyway, mostly because, on his Twitter feed and at his ongoing campaign rallies, he has fed them a steady diet of entertaining, rhetorical red meat. They love his feistiness, how he never apologizes, how he stands up for their values, and how he sticks it to his enemies every day. They know all his lines, and still thrill to hear him deliver them. They feel that he relates to them and call him "the blue-collar billionaire." One important question for 2020, as well as the 2018 midterm elections, will be the extent to which Trump's appeal is grounded in a larger movement or whether it is based more on a cult of personality.

Trump's historically low approval ratings have been inching up recently, into the low forties. And those ratings likely don't reflect all his support, since many national polls survey eligible voters rather than registered or likely voters. Plus, as the 2016 election proved, Trump probably still has a hidden vote that pollsters are not capturing because some people remain embarrassed to admit that they like him.

To win back Trump voters in Luzerne County and many places like it around the country, Democrats will need to more clearly define what they are for, rather than who and what they are against: Trump the man and everything he stands for.

And the party, whose base has shifted away from the working class to the middle, upper-middle, professional, and creative classes, will need to make more room for centrist voices if it wants to reach voters who now feel culturally alienated from its prevailing liberal orthodoxy.

In addition, the Democratic Party, which has long prided itself on its tolerance, will have to curb the tendency of many of its leaders to use a broad brush to paint most Trump voters as bigots.

The real issue was that they felt deeply aggrieved— aggrieved by a government and political class they believe abandoned them or left them marginalized in a new economy, and by a dominant liberal culture that condescends to them and mocks their way of life.

They had felt forgotten and wanted to be respected. Then Trump came along and seemed to recognize and acknowledge them. He made them feel good about themselves, while Hillary made them feel ashamed. So they voted for Trump. It basically all came down to that.

"People fall in love with their therapist because they want to be heard, and they want to be heard without judgment," says Tiffany Cloud. "I think people felt Donald Trump heard them without judgment."

ACKNOWLEDGMENTS

I want to thank the dozen people who served as the main characters and voices of *The Forgotten:* the Trump Men—Vito DeLuca, Ed Harry, Marty Beccone, and Brian Langan; the Trump Women—Lynette Villano, Donna Kowalczyk, Kim Woodrosky, and Tiffany Cloud; as well as Congressman Lou Barletta, Erik Olson, Steve Smith, and Jessica Harker.

They selflessly gave hours of their time, with little apparent suspicion, to a writer from a blue state and proved that dialogue in a divided land is more than possible. They expressed varying degrees of support for and allegiance to Donald Trump, but all provided me with enlightening commentary on their motivations in voting for the president. They carefully and candidly explained the underlying reasons for Trump's appeal to them and for the Trump phenomenon as they saw it. I learned a lot from each of them.

Thanks also to the local Democrats I interviewed in opposition—Amilcar Arroyo; Ben Medina; Ron Felton; Alicia Mendoza Watkinson and her sister, Amanda Mendoza; as well as Johanna Habib Czarnecki and her daughter, Alia Habib—who described what it's like to live amid the triumphant Trumpers in Luzerne County these days.

I also want to thank Ray Harker, Jessica's husband, whose

willingness to discuss with me Trump's effect on their marriage with such honesty and candor made him a key player in Jess's story. While Jess thinks Trump was sent by God, Ray thinks he was sent by Satan. In an extreme way, the Harkers' story illustrates the divisive impact that Trump's election has had on many American families.

Special thanks also to Charles McElwee, a talented writer and Luzerne County historian, who, for his day job, works as an economic development specialist for the nonprofit Community Area New Development Organization in Hazleton, Pennsylvania. Charles read drafts of the introduction and the "Luzerne" chapter and provided helpful suggestions and critiques. He also provided research assistance on several topics.

Tony Brooks, a Wilkes-Barre city councilman and noted local historian, provided me with helpful historical guidance on Wilkes-Barre and the county as well.

Thank you also to:

Luzerne County manager Dave Pedri; Luzerne County's representatives in the Pennsylvania legislature: representatives Eddie Pashinski and Aaron Kaufer, and state senators John Yudichak and Tarah Toohil; Luzerne County district attorney Stefanie Salavantis; Luzerne County coroner Bill Lisman; Cathy Ryzner, a recovery specialist at Wyoming Valley Alcohol and Drug Services in Wilkes-Barre; Bob Curry, director of the Hazleton Integration Project; Krista Schneider, executive director of the Downtown Hazleton Alliance for Progress; Sue Henry, the former Wilkes-Barre radio talk show host; Mark Riccetti Jr., director of operations at the Luzerne County Historical Society; reporter Bill O'Boyle of the *Times Leader* newspaper in Wilkes-Barre and his former executive editor Tim Farkas; Shannon Monnat, former assistant professor of rural sociology, demography, and sociology at Penn State University and current associate professor of sociology at Syracuse University; Margaret Phillips, a retired phone company executive who lives in Dallas, outside Wilkes-Barre, and is an ardent Trump supporter; and Diane Hessan, an entrepreneur and author in Boston who has been in conversation with four hundred voters nationally across the political spectrum since the 2016 election.

Thanks to my old friend Geoff Shandler, the editor of my biography on Ted Williams, *The Kid,* who expressed an early interest in this project, discussed themes with me, and even suggested the title.

Thank you to John Parsley, who acquired *The Forgotten* for Little, Brown but then left before we had a chance to work together. Vanessa Mobley inherited me but never made me feel like I was a hand-me-down. She was enthused about the book from the start and gave me expert editing. Thanks also to Vanessa's able assistant, Joseph Lee, and to Little, Brown publisher Reagan Arthur for keeping me in-house following *The Kid.*

I am grateful to the estimable Nell Beram for her skillful copyediting job, as well as to Little, Brown senior production editor Ben Allen and executive production editor Karen Landry.

Thanks to my agent, Joe Veltre of Gersh, for deftly negotiating all the particulars.

Thank you also to my old pals at the *Boston Globe*—Sam Allis, Steve Kurkjian, Mike Rezendes, Charlie Sennott,

Walter Robinson, Mitch Zuckoff, and Brian McGrory—who were interested in the book and often suggested ideas.

Thanks to my three wonderful kids—Greta Bradlee Williams, Joe Bradlee, and Anna Bradlee—who are always there for me. And, finally, thanks to my fabulous wife, Cynthia, who embraced the book, cheered me on, and delighted in reading selected chapters while offering insightful commentary on the characters.

My apologies to anyone I have inadvertently forgotten.

NOTES

INTRODUCTION

1 Samantha Cooney, "These Are the Women Who Have Accused President Trump of Sexual Misconduct," *Time,* December 12, 2017.

2 Sources on exit polls: Alec Tyson and Shiva Maniam, "Behind Trump's Victory: Divisions by Race, Gender, and Education," Pew Research Center, November 9, 2016; Chris Cillizza, "The Thirteen Most Amazing Findings in the 2016 Exit Poll," *Washington Post,* November 10, 2016; Nate Cohn, "A 2016 Review: Turnout Wasn't the Driver of Clinton's Defeat," *New York Times,* March 28, 2017.

3 Emily Ekins, "The Five Types of Trump Voters: Who They Are and What They Believe," Democracy Fund Voter Study Group, June 2017.

4 Peggy Noonan, "Trump and the Rise of the Unprotected," *Wall Street Journal,* February 25, 2016.

5 Charles F. McElwee III, "Morton Downey Jr. Hosted the Original Trump Rally—Thirty Years Ago," *American Conservative,* October 2, 2017.

6 Jeff Greenfield, "Trump Is Pat Buchanan with Better Timing," *Politico,* September/October 2016.

LUZERNE

1 Charles F. McElwee III, "Slow Fade of the Pennsylvania Irish," *American Conservative,* February 15, 2018.

2 Charles F. McElwee III, "In 1880, Hazleton Banker's Surprise Vote Put James Garfield on GOP Ballot," *Hazleton Standard-Speaker,* July 17, 2016.

3 Edward F. Hanlon, *The Wyoming Valley: An American Portrait* (Woodland Hills, CA: Windsor Publications, 1983), 155.

4 Bob Davis and John W. Miller, "The Places That Made Donald Trump President," *Wall Street Journal,* November 11, 2016.

5 Michele Norris, "As America Changes, Some Anxious Whites Feel Left Behind," *National Geographic,* April 2018.

6 *Tucker Carlson Tonight,* Fox News, March 20, 2018.

7 As quoted in Thomas B. Edsall, "How Fear of Falling Explains the Love of Trump," *New York Times,* July 20, 2017.

8 *Language Log,* November 17, 2007.

9 YouTube video on Heynabonics (https://video.search.yahoo.com/yhs/search?fr=yhs-GenieoYaho-fh_hp&hsimp=yhs-fh_hp&hspart=GenieoYaho&p=heynabonics#id=1&vid=568445d0df8c9aa68fd0b6c4f0b16f6e&action=click).

10 Anne Case and Sir Angus Deaton, "Mortality and Morbidity in the Twenty-First Century," Brookings Papers on Economic Activity, March 23, 2017.

THE WHITE NATIONALIST

1 Heidi Beirich and Susy Buchanan, "2017: The Year in Hate and Extremism," Southern Poverty Law Center, February 11, 2018.

2 Ibid.

3 Ibid.

4 Jerry Lynott, "Ku Klux Klan Recruiting in Northeast Pennsylvania for a New Era," *Times Leader,* October 17, 2015.

5 Betsy Woodruff, "Skinheads Come Out in Full Force for Donald Trump in Pennsylvania," *Daily Beast,* April 26, 2016.

6 Leah Nelson, "Longtime White Supremacist to Serve on Pennsylvania County GOP Committee," Southern Poverty Law Center, May 30, 2012.

7 Ibid.

8 Michael P. Buffer, "Republicans Ponder Ousting Skinhead from Committee," *Citizens' Voice,* June 5, 2012.

9 Charlotte L. Jacobson, "Community Unites Against Racism at Swoyersville Rally," *Citizens' Voice,* November 2, 2015.

10 Michael P. Buffer, "'White Rights Advocate' Wins Second Term on County's Republican Committee," *Citizens' Voice,* April 29, 2016.

THE CHRISTIAN

1 Amy Sullivan, "Democrats Are Christians, Too," *New York Times,* March 31, 2018.

THE CONGRESSMAN (REPRISE)

1 Jenna Johnson, "Donald Trump Is in a Funk: Bitter, Hoarse, and Pondering, 'If I Lose...'" *Washington Post,* October 21, 2016.

2 Jenna Johnson and Jose A. DelReal, "In Historic Gettysburg, Lincoln Spoke of Unity; Trump Complained of a 'Totally Rigged' System," *Washington Post,* October 22, 2016.

THE DEMOCRATS

1 Alia Hanna Habib, "To Understand the Rust Belt, We Need to See Beyond Whiteness," *BuzzFeed,* January 12, 2017.

EPILOGUE

1 Tim Alberta, "Social Conservatives Are 'Over the Moon' about Trump," *Politico,* April 26, 2017; and Eugene Scott, "White Evangelicals' Support of Trump Holding Steady," CNN, April 28, 2017.

2 Jeffrey Goldberg, "A Senior White House Official Describes the Trump Doctrine: 'We're America, Bitch,'" *The Atlantic,* June 11, 2018.

3 Quinnipiac University survey of 1,106 voters, January 5–9, 2018.

4 Doug Sosnik, "Trump Is on Track to Win Reelection," *Washington Post,* October 6, 2017.

5 Thomas B. Edsall, "Democrats Are Playing Checkers While Trump Is Playing Chess," *New York Times,* October 12, 2017.

6 *Washington Post* staff, "What Trump Proposed Cutting in His 2019 Budget," *Washington Post,* February 12, 2018.

BIBLIOGRAPHY

Allen, Jonathan, and Amie Parnes. *Shattered: Inside Hillary Clinton's Doomed Campaign*. New York: Crown, 2017.

Anderson, Carol. *White Rage: The Unspoken Truth of Our Racial Divide*. New York: Bloomsbury, 2016.

Bishop, Bill. *The Big Sort: Why the Clustering of Like-Minded America Is Tearing Us Apart*. Boston: Mariner Books, 2009.

Blair, Gwenda. *The Trumps: Three Generations That Built an Empire*. New York: Simon and Schuster, 2000.

Coates, Ta-Nehisi. *We Were Eight Years in Power: An American Tragedy*. New York: One World Publishing, 2017.

D'Antonio, Michael. *Never Enough: Donald Trump and the Pursuit of Success*. New York: Thomas Dunne Books, 2015.

Dionne, E. J., Jr., Norman J. Ornstein, and Thomas E. Mann. *One Nation After Trump: A Guide for the Perplexed, the Disillusioned, the Desperate, and the Not-Yet Deported*. New York: St. Martin's Press, 2017.

Green, Joshua. *Devil's Bargain: Steve Bannon, Donald Trump, and the Storming of the Presidency*. New York: Penguin Press, 2017.

Hochschild, Arlie Russell. *Strangers in Their Own Land: Anger and Mourning on the American Right*. New York: The New Press, 2016.

Isenberg, Nancy. *White Trash: The 400-Year Untold History of Class in America*. New York: Viking Press, 2016.

Kranish, Michael, and Marc Fisher. *Trump Revealed: The Definitive Biography of the 45th President*. New York: Scribner, 2016.

Lewandowski, Corey R., and David N. Bossie. *Let Trump Be Trump: The Inside Story of His Rise to the Presidency*. New York: Center Street, 2017.

Lewis, Sinclair. *It Can't Happen Here*. New York: Signet Classics, 2014.

Longazel, Jamie. *Undocumented Fears: Immigration and the Politics of Di-*

vide and Conquer in Hazleton, Pennsylvania. Philadelphia: Temple University Press, 2016.

Murray, Charles. *Coming Apart: The State of White America, 1960–2010.* New York: Crown Forum, 2012.

Olson, Tiffany Cloud. *Sleeping with Dog Tags.* Tarentum, PA: Word Association Publishers, 2012.

Packer, George. *The Unwinding: An Inner History of the New America.* New York: Farrar, Straus and Giroux, 2013.

Patterson, Richard North. *Fever Swamp: A Journey Through the Strange Neverland of the 2016 Presidential Race.* New York: Quercus, 2017.

Quinones, Sam. *Dreamland: The True Tale of America's Opiate Epidemic.* New York: Bloomsbury Press, 2015.

Sexton, Jared Yates. *The People Are Going to Rise Like the Waters Upon Your Shore: A Story of American Rage.* Berkeley: Counterpoint, 2017.

Stone, Roger. *The Making of the President 2016: How Donald Trump Orchestrated a Revolution.* New York: Skyhorse Publishing, 2017.

Taibbi, Matt. *Insane Clown President: Dispatches from the 2016 Circus.* New York: Spiegel and Grau, 2017.

Trump, Donald J., with Tony Schwartz. *Trump: The Art of the Deal.* New York: Random House, 1987.

Tur, Katy. *Unbelievable: My Front-Row Seat to the Craziest Campaign in American History.* New York: Dey Street Books, 2017.

Vance, J. D. *Hillbilly Elegy: A Memoir of a Family and Culture in Crisis.* New York: Harper, 2016.

Wick, Harrison. *Images of America: Luzerne County.* Charleston: Arcadia Publishing, 2011.

Williams, Joan C. *White Working Class: Overcoming Class Cluelessness in America.* Boston: Harvard Business Review Press, 2017.

Wolff, Michael. *Fire and Fury: Inside the Trump White House.* New York: Henry Holt and Company, 2018.

Young, Kevin. *Bunk: The Rise of Hoaxes, Humbug, Plagiarists, Phonies, Post-Facts, and Fake News.* Minneapolis: Graywolf Press, 2017.

Zito, Salena, and Brad Todd. *The Great Revolt: Inside the Populist Coalition Reshaping American Politics.* New York: Crown Forum, 2018.

ABOUT THE AUTHOR

Ben Bradlee Jr. is the author of the critically acclaimed *The Kid: The Immortal Life of Ted Williams* (2013) and three other books. Bradlee spent twenty-five years as a reporter and editor for the *Boston Globe* and, as deputy managing editor, oversaw the *Globe*'s Pulitzer Prize–winning coverage of the sexual abuse scandal in the Catholic Church from July 2001 to August 2002. He lives outside Boston.